# The Art of Influence

RYUHO OKAWA

BOOKS

IRH PRESS

New York

Library of Congress Cataloging-in-Publication Data

ISBN 13: 978-1-942125-48-8

ISBN 10: 1-942125-48-8

Printed in Canada

First Edition

Book Design: Jess Morphew

Cover / Interior Image © L.DEP / Shutterstock.com

# The Art of Influence

## 28 WAYS TO WIN PEOPLE'S HEARTS AND BRING POSITIVE CHANGE TO YOUR LIFE

# RYUHO OKAWA

IRH PRESS

# Contents

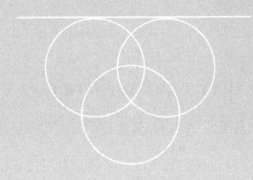

CHAPTER TWO

# How to Become an Influential Leader

CHAPTER THREE

# How to Overcome Stress

## I. THE ART OF ACHIEVING SUCCESS WITH A CALM MIND

# PREFACE

If you read this book carefully and thoroughly, you will see that I'm not a mere leader of a new religion like the mass media like to portray me. The unbounded and independent spirit that dominates this book shows that I am a modern philosopher who speaks in living language, as well as a thinker and leader of the times.

You'll also see that I am a master of the spiritual world who mentors and guides many business executives and leaders around the world. I sense that I'm becoming the "spirit of the times," in the Hegelian sense, for both Japan and the larger world.

This book will surely mark a new beginning of your life and the world surrounding you.

Ryuho Okawa
Founder and CEO
Happy Science

CHAPTER ONE

# *How to Build* Mental Toughness

# I.

# *The* Art *of* Mastering Relationships

# 1. Learning from Other People's Advice and Opinions

**QUESTION**

How can I be more open to other people's advice and opinions?

## ANSWER

*"Cultivating a wish to learn from others is the first necessary step."*

The ability to open your mind to other people's advice and opinions is important. My first recommendation is to ensure that you are willing to learn from others, because the lack of a desire to learn from others is what prevents us from listening to their advice. If you have a habit of tuning out other people's advice, it's often because your strong but unrecognized egotism and pride are leading you to resist other people's opinions. So cultivating a wish to learn from others is the first necessary step.

If you find that you're eager to learn from others, then my second recommendation is to look at the positive aspects rather than the negative aspects of those who come to you with their advice. Their social status, gender, and age shouldn't make a difference in how you receive their opinions. Many precious life lessons may slip through your fingers if you allow your prejudices to close you off to those who have less wealth, status, or education than others; those who are younger; or those with other types of attributes. If you allow someone's impressive position or status or the lack of those things to determine whom you choose to lend your ears to, you'll limit the wealth of learning opportunities available to you in life.

This is why it's crucial to cultivate a wish to learn from anyone and everyone who offers positive seeds to nourish your soul. If you're truly determined to learn from others, you should earnestly learn from their perspectives to gain valuable lessons from them.

*"Share with others the beneficial advice that you've received in the past."*

My third piece of advice is to not let yourself disregard other people's advice and suggestions, and instead find a way to incorporate it into your day-to-day life.

And a fourth important thing you can do is share with others the beneficial advice that you've received in the past. There are many things about ourselves that we don't notice, so by listening to others' advice, we may find opportunities that dramatically shift the course of our lives. If someone you know is suffering from a problem like one you've faced before, the tried and tested advice that helped you may benefit this person. Sharing your wisdom with others in this way lets you act with true selfless compassion and practice a great human virtue.

> *"We need to learn to distinguish between what we do have control over from what we don't."*

Let me tell you about a time in my life when listening to someone's advice helped me. When I was working in the corporate world, someone once said something to me that taught me a valuable lesson: There may be things in life that we can control, but there are also things in life that lie beyond our power to change.

This is what this person said to me: "Is the problem that's on your mind right now an issue that lies within or outside your control? An issue that's within your power to change certainly deserves your best effort. But if you find that there's nothing within your power that can help, then there are times when you'll need to acknowledge that it's beyond your control and let the problem pass." This advice taught me an important, new mindset.

Many of us spend much of our lives dwelling on problems we have no control over, while we neglect problems that our efforts can help solve. What can we possibly achieve in life if we keep trying to solve problems that we have no power over? We need to learn to distinguish between what we do have control over from what we don't and to put the latter aside.

This is why I have taught myself to follow these steps when I am faced with life's issues: First, I determine which things are within my power to change, and then I try to solve the problem by improving myself. Then, with respect to things that lie outside my own control, I learn as much as I can from them and then set them aside, at least for the time being. Some of them will resolve over time, and others may not. Whatever the outcomes, this is how I've learned to look at my issues. And this is one way of thinking that has helped me lead a successful life.

*"Our own emotions are fully within our power to control."*

Other people's feelings are a prime example of things that lie beyond our individual power to control. No matter what we do, we can't change the feelings that other people experience. The best we can do is offer them our advice, but we can't always make them change things about themselves.

In contrast, our own emotions are fully within our power to control. Even in the middle of an argument with a friend, your thoughts and feelings are always open to your own choices. Even in a heated moment, it's up to the free will of none other than yourself to decide how you think and feel about your friend. Do you wish to spend ten years harboring resentment in your heart and speaking ill words about your friend? Or do you wish to forgive and forget the argument the next day? It's completely up to you.

So when you've finished telling your friend everything there is to tell, and you're certain that there's nothing else you can possibly do or say to help, you need to believe in the power of your words to nourish your friend's soul and eventually bring him or her to the positive path. What's important is that you become the master of your own thoughts and emotions.

> *"The more your store of inner
> wisdom is allowed to develop,
> the more extraordinary
> your character will become."*

I've now discussed four points that will help you open your mind to other people's advice and opinions, to which I would like to add an additional point. When you practice the advice you receive, find it beneficial, and then share with others this wisdom you've gained, you gain an additional learning experience to add to the store of the wisdom within your soul. In the end, the more your store of inner wisdom is allowed to develop, the more extraordinary your character will become.

# 2. Respecting Boundaries

**QUESTION**

How can I build good relationships
at home and in the workplace?

## ANSWER

*"We need to honor and respect the professional boundaries that exist in the workplace."*

When we're at work, we may not always agree with our superior's decisions, and we may hesitate to say so. We fear that our words could be seen as a sign of disrespect and put our job at risk. In such a situation, an effective principle for cultivating smooth relationships is to acknowledge the difference between each other's positions or roles.

This principle is about honoring the differences between other workers' positions and your own to maintain harmony and order in your workplace. People who highly value righteousness may feel justified in approaching others as equals and behaving similarly to everyone, regardless of differing organizational ranks. You may believe that once you and your superior are in the boxing ring, there is nothing that separates you from each other; even if you are just a junior boxer and he is a grand champion, you think of yourself as one fighter pitted against another fighter, in the end. But this approach to your workplace relationships is a sure recipe for failure to move up in the world.

Honoring the boundaries between others' positions and your own and knowing how to approach each person accordingly is vital to your career success and is also the secret to career longevity. When you need to tell your superior that his decision could be a grave mistake, it's crucial to first consider how best to approach your superior in a respectful way. Bringing up a sensitive subject while acting as though you're his equal in position can only lead to failure.

Whether it's with our superiors or our subordinates, we need to honor and respect the professional boundaries that exist in the workplace. For example, if you're in the position of division manager, you'll need to speak with an attitude of respect toward the general manager, especially if you want to offer criticism. Treating your superior as though you hold the same corporate rank could seem disrespectful in light of basic workplace principles, and this may lead to losing your job in the end.

> *"Don't allow personal feelings of like or dislike prevent you from associating with different people."*

Many seasoned professional men in the business world have, at least to some degree, learned to respect professional boundaries, while some women with less experience find it more difficult to grasp the idea. They may fall into an all-or-nothing approach in building workplace relationships, becoming prone to either attaching to or completely detaching from people, depending on the individual. It's easier to build relationships with those they feel a strong connection with, and it's harder to do this when there's no connection at all. This puts them at risk of poor workplace relationships and discord.

My advice, in this case, is to not allow personal feelings of like or dislike to prevent you from associating with different people, and to instead determine the appropriate kind of professional relationship and make a mental note of the boundaries to respect. Doing so can help these relationships work more smoothly.

The difference between our professional and personal lives is also a topic we naturally need to think about. Some women may mix workplace and personal relationships and feel content using their personal likes and dislikes to judge people, but this risks inviting a lot of unnecessary conflict with others. If you recognize this habit in yourself, you may find useful hints for improving your workplace relationships by observing how men build professional relationships in the workplace.

> *"Respecting each other's boundaries can mean the difference between family peace and utter discord."*

The same approach can help prevent marital conflicts. Instead of unleashing unhindered wrath upon each other or resorting to living separately to stay out of each other's sight, showing respect for each other's boundaries, even during an argument, can prevent many married couples from taking the path of the "war to end all wars."

The same can be said in parent-child relationships. Respecting each other's boundaries can mean the difference between family peace and utter discord. In the wake of a brewing conflict with your parents, you can practice reminding yourself that your parents' lives will not last forever, and they may no longer be here come several decades down the road. Remembering this can help you a lot when you're struggling to manage your own emotions while doing the best you can to listen to what your parents want to say. It's when we forget that the days of our parents' lives are numbered and that they're not going to be with us forever that we let our emotions and frustrations get the better of us.

A lack of respect for each other's boundaries is also the cause of conflict between many wives and their mothers-in-law, particularly in Japan where I am from. Relationships often get strained when the mother-in-law steps in and gets too involved in matters that should stay between her son and daughter-in-law. Often, when the mother-in-law intrudes upon their relationship in this way, all chaos breaks loose. But by respecting her daughter-in-law's role as her son's wife and allowing her daughter-in-law to have the closest relationship with him, which is no more than the daughter-in-law deserves, the mother-in-law allows her daughter-in-law to trust her and rely on her as a confidant.

Whether at the workplace or in the home, respecting one another's boundaries is an important, harmonizing relationship principle to follow.

# 3. Developing the Power of Persuasion

## QUESTION

How can I persuade my superior
at work who is much older and refuses
to accept my ideas?

# ANSWER

## "Work on refining your charm."

Societies in Japan and around the world have to some degree been built on a system of seniority. So the experience of working under a superior who's much older than you is one that's widely shared by many people. Many organizations have relied on age as a useful way of knowing a worker's job capability because of how little we can tell just from the outside. This is why many institutions have incorporated seniority systems to promote harmony and order.

Older superiors' refusing to accept their subordinates' ideas, then, is a naturally occurring challenge. Superiors are often bracing themselves, determined not to give in too easily to their subordinates' ideas. So what can you do under these circumstances, when you face a very obvious age gap between you and your superior?

The first piece of advice I can give you is to work on refining your charm. A charming personality can inspire your superior to help you to get a leg up in the world. With a charming personality, you can make your superiors want to listen to and help you, even if you're much younger than them. The key is to make your superior say, "All right, I give in. You've won me over."

So what can you do to build a charming personality? Ultimately, charm comes through in your personality: in the way you think, perceive, and carry yourself in the presence of others. If you've ever carefully observed someone who is young but has gained the love and affection of many of her elders, you've seen an endearing air about her that puts others at ease and makes them want to open their hearts to her. This endearing aura is a very important element of charm.

*"Refrain from appearing presumptuous."*

If you don't want to leave your superior with an impression of you as cheeky, I recommend avoiding behaving brazenly toward him, since this can turn them away. Your superior, I'm sure, is aware that many good ideas exist that he may not have come up with yet, but he isn't about to accept all the ideas you think up, even if you've proved how intelligent you are, and it's normal for your superior to think in this way.

So for my second piece of advice, I recommend refraining from appearing presumptuous and instead being conscious that you're in a subordinate position to your superior, still lack experience, and have much more to learn about important things. As long as you have this basic mindset as the basis of your intentions, I think you'll do fine when approaching your superior with your ideas. And when you do, allow your superior to see that you have made an effort to understand his idea and are presenting an additional approach. Lead your superior into seeing how your ideas could be successful without making him feel as though he's being persuaded or willfully lured into your opinions.

> *"Gain your superior's understanding of your unique personality and character."*

Another way of persuading your superior is to first get her to understand your character and then use this as a basis for communicating and behaving in your own way. For example, if you're known to be blunt with your words but kind and thoughtful at heart, then show your superior that you have these character traits. Understanding your unique personality traits will give your superior a basis for listening to and accepting your ideas.

We humans cannot agree with other people's opinions as willingly when they come from people we have difficulty understanding. We put up a strong defense against those we aren't capable of fully comprehending. This is why gaining your superior's understanding of your unique personality and character is a very important element of winning your superior's acceptance.

> ## *"Show how eager you are to learn from your superior."*

Last but not least, it's also important that you feel fond of your superior and wish to learn as much as you can from him. We humans willingly open our hearts to people who think well of us and show a willingness to learn from us. So it's important to cultivate a fondness for your superior. If you show how eager you are to learn from your superior as you spend time with him, you're certain to open up an opportunity to present your discoveries.

Older people feel delighted when younger people look up to them and depend on them, so by showing how much you rely on their instructions, you're encouraging them to gladly listen to you in turn. To sum up, what's most important is that you come one step down in your attitude when you approach those who are senior to you, as you make your way toward presenting them your ideas and opinions.

# II.

# *The* Art *of* Actualizing Your Dreams *and* Ideals

# 4. Developing Your Capabilities

### QUESTION

A lot of times, when our life circumstances change, it gives us new perspectives and opportunities for growth. When I find that I can't develop my capabilities in my current circumstance, what should I do?

## ANSWER

> *"Your circumstances will change
> if you change yourself."*

There may not be a straightforward answer to your question. What I mean is that the circumstances we face now basically change as a result of improving our own capability. So making changes to our current circumstances is not the only means to improve our work capabilities. Developing our capabilities while we're still in our current environment will also bring definite changes to the circumstances that surround us.

For example, someone who has been working in the same department for a decade or more and has successfully overcome her shortcomings and built up her strengths, would have definitely seen her circumstances change. People above her would have taken notice of her as a highly capable person, and the circumstances she's in now should look different than before.

People in higher positions don't want unchallenged, capable workers to continue working on the same things in the same place. So if you are struggling because of your current environment, it may be a sign that your weaknesses and strengths need further improvement. Changing your current circumstances will sometimes bring opportunities to change yourself. But it's crucial to know that your circumstances will change if you change yourself, and there is a definite mutual influence at work between you and your surroundings.

> *"Companies need employees who produce value that far exceeds their salaries."*

Employers sometimes send employees who have the potential to be generalists through a range of departments to give them a wide range of experiences. This provides very valuable experiences that these workers will be thankful for.

After being moved around to many departments, workers who lack positive results will settle into one department to develop specialized skills there. They'll continue to hold their job as long as they produce value that exceeds their salary, and when this value falls below their salary, they may face demotion or a salary reduction, or they may even be let go. Whereas, those who continue to be moved around are seen having the potential for managerial positions and are being counted on to develop the skills of a generalist. This is how things work in many organizations. This system makes sense when you see it from the perspective of whether you are taking love or giving love to others through your work.

To run their businesses, companies need employees who produce value that far exceeds their salaries. Running a business involves many expenses besides the salaries of all the rest of the employees, such as rent, electricity, water, and office supplies. So the value that one worker with, for example, a $20,000 salary needs to produce when all these expenses are accounted for totals $100,000 or more. But many employees who are not aware of these economics are satisfied with continuing to produce the value they're producing now.

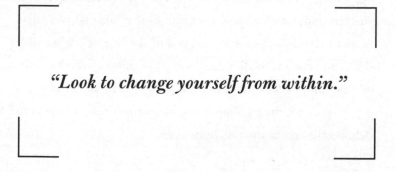

*"Look to change yourself from within."*

Since I founded Happy Science back in 1986, I've seen many changes in my circumstances and environment. Happy Science, the world, and other aspects of my surroundings have gone through changes that have necessarily led to shifts in my own self-awareness. My new self-awareness has, in turn, helped me put out new work into the world, resulting in new changes to my surroundings. This cycle of continuous change has led me to become the person that I am today. And just as I am not the same person that I was several decades ago, you're no longer the same person that you used to be several years ago.

It can be difficult to improve your capabilities in an environment that never changes. Usually, people in this situation eventually find a different place to move on to. But if you'd still like to stay where you are, my advice is to look to change yourself from within. Even if your current environment remains static, by deepening your inner world and broadening your introspection, you can cultivate useful power for your future. You will, of course, need to develop more knowledge and develop thoughts with depth and cultivation. But developing the ability to think deeply on new things is also a type of change that can be achieved.

In the end, though, improving your capabilities will lead to definite changes in your circumstances.

# 5. Shifting the Course of Your Destiny

**QUESTION**

You've said before that we're all born
with a life plan that we created
before we set out for this world.
Is it possible for us to make changes
to this plan as we live our lives
in this world?

# ANSWER

## "Our original life plans can indeed be altered."

Just as we each have a different personality, we each created our life plan in a different way. Some of us are born with very detailed plans, while others have rough plans, some of which only say where and to whom we want to be born and leave everything else up to circumstances. The souls with this less specific kind of life plan often came here just hoping to have fun. The reason for this difference more or less lies in the differences in our soul levels—that is, the degrees of spiritual progress that our souls have reached. For the greater your mission is in this life, the more detailed your soul's life plan often is.

The course of destiny does change, however, and our original life plans can indeed be altered. Our conditions and circumstances constantly shift as we live our lives in this world, and those changes may bring us more meaningful soul-training experiences than those we originally planned. This can happen when we underestimate the level of progress our souls will make. Over the course of decades of effort in this life, we might get further ahead than we had imagined. Sure enough, the opposite sometimes happens too: sometimes, the goals we set before birth were too high for us to reach, and so we have to downshift.

But when souls have underestimated their potential, their original plan isn't necessarily the best course for them to take. It's more important that they shift their goals higher, so as not to let this opportunity go to waste. And by doing so, they'll invite the best assistance that their guardian and guiding spirits can give them.

> *"Cultivating inner virtue can turn the course of your fate in a positive direction when a supporter appears into your life."*

Another determining factor that can change the course of your destiny is other people's influence; we are not the sole determiners of our fate. The course of your life's destiny is also tremendously affected by the impact of other people's influence.

I've heard that people in China greet one another by asking whether they've met a nobleman recently or by wishing for them to encounter one in the near future. This greeting comes from their belief that people with the power to bring us good fortune exist, and I also believe that such people exist.

There is almost nothing in this world that can't be achieved by gaining support of various people. By gaining people's strong support, you can achieve, with ease, goals and dreams that are beyond what you can accomplish by struggling alone.

So what sort of conditions do we need to fulfill to attract such supporters? The answer to this question has to do with our virtues.

Cultivating inner virtue can turn the course of your fate in a positive direction when a supporter appears into your life. But even when someone appears, you may find yourself straying toward the opposite, downward path if you lack virtue. This happens more often than we would like to believe. Making the wrong decision during a key turning point could send you down a sinking path, and you could spend five or ten years bouncing back from it until another chance arrives. When this second chance does arrive, we all hope that we'll make the right choices to lead us on the path upward, but some people will choose the path that takes them further downward.

In this way, some lives keep sinking downward while others

turn around and climb higher. These undulations are the result of our decisions during each vital turning point in our lives, for life swings to and fro between good times and bad times.

> *"Where your destiny leads in this life depends a lot on your spiritual training and efforts."*

Where your destiny leads in this life depends a lot on your spiritual training and efforts. In addition, your guardian and guiding spirits' guidance and other people's support will also influence your life significantly. In the end, your power to attract both of these things to you depends on how deeply you've cultivated your virtues through effort.

The course of your life is strewn with a number of turning points. Your ability to guide yourself to the positive path at each turning point depends on your day-to-day efforts to polish your virtue and develop your capacity. Guidance will come to those who make this effort and who shine with an inner light, and this guidance will give you great power in your life.

The teachings of Happy Science offer a high-level perspective on life that experts on life think of. These teachings will, when followed, greatly increase your potential to shift the course of your life upward.

I hope you'll make the effort to change your destiny. It's definitely possible to shift the course of your destiny. If your wish aligns with the wishes of the guiding spirits above your guardian spirit, you can shift the course of your fate toward an even greater life scenario than you'd originally planned.

# 6. Persevering through Hardship

## QUESTION

I have continued to hold onto my dreams in my mind. But some of these dreams have turned into painful obsessions, because they aren't getting any closer to being realized.
What can I do to get past this?

## ANSWER

> *"If your will is pointed in the right direction, your dream will definitely become reality."*

In the course of realizing your dreams, the most important, key thing you must do as part of your spiritual training in this world is patiently endure the passing of time. I've previously said that perseverance plays an important role in spreading the Truths,* and I still believe this to be true.

If your will is pointed in the right direction as you endure the passage of time, your dream will definitely become reality; this is how dreams and ideals become fulfilled. If, however, your strong wish to achieve your dream has been fruitless and you're painfully attached to it and impatient, then you're not undergoing your spiritual training in the correct way.

If this has been your struggle, consider looking within yourself to see where your dream is issuing from—is it coming

---

* I discussed this topic in *On Boundless Love*. The original Japanese title of this book is *Mugen No Ai To Wa Nanika* (Tokyo: IRH Press, 1992).

from the depths of your soul or from someplace shallower? We often don't realize this, but it's for the sake of our happiness that our wrong desires remain unfulfilled. We wish for many things to happen, believing that heaven shares our wishes. But in many cases, when we look back on our earlier wishes, we realize that it was for the better that they didn't come true.

> *"If you find that your dream is different from heaven's will, you'll need to accept heaven's wish as your fate."*

Your ability to determine whether or not your dream aligns with heaven's wish will depend largely on your degree of awareness in this present moment. You'll need to judge where heaven's will lies by looking objectively at the results of your efforts and perseverance.

If you find that your dream is different from heaven's will, you'll need to accept heaven's wish as your fate. As humans, we inevitably have wrong desires. Even if you're certain that you've pored through enough information to lead you to the right decision at that time, some years later you may find that a much better road was possible than the one you had wished for.

So as I said earlier, being mindful of patiently enduring the passage of time is an important part of living with right will. It's within this spiritual training that heaven's will is revealed, so when it does, you don't want to misread it. If you ever find that heaven's will is pointing in a different direction, you need to be brave and realign your course.

> *"Our souls are polished through the variety of experiences we gain."*

If you're learning the Truths at Happy Science, it's safe to say that your guardian spirit is spiritually awake and watching over you, and that means that you probably haven't veered in a grievously bad direction. There are times when it's important to be willing to simply go wherever life takes you. When thinking hard about an issue seems to lead you nowhere, that may be the time to leave your fate up to your guardian spirit, while you continue making efforts, day by day, persevering over the course of half a year, one year, two years, and then three years, accumulating your efforts over time. By continuing to move forward in this way, you'll be able to see the right direction to head in.

There's no end to the number of people who panic, just steps before they arrive at their destination. In their panic, they flounder and wander off in an odd direction, treading straight down the wrong path. These are the times when you need to have grit. We can say that building your grit is a synonym for soul training.

The purpose of life in this world is to polish our souls, and that means that not all of life is going to bring joyful experiences. Our souls are polished through the variety of experiences we gain. If you can continue to believe that you are a rough diamond that's being polished, and continue to persevere under every circumstance, this time of difficulty will eventually pass and open a new path before you.

You can't polish a diamond's surfaces using tofu or jello. Diamonds need something much harder than them to make them shine. When something extremely hard befalls you, then, it's a sure sign of the hard diamond that exists within you. The scale of the hardships that befall you is equivalent to the hardness of the inner diamond of your soul.

If you look at your hardship as offering the right level of grit for your inner diamond, you'll understand that this, too, shall pass, and there's no need to set time limits on your dreams. As you continue on in this way, you'll see the currents of your life as if you stood atop a hill, from a higher perspective, watching over the river of life below you.

What is vital is to develop inner grit. The greatest failures and mistakes are sometimes our blessings. They make our smaller mistakes much easier to bear and overcome, and they give us the perspective to see that our smaller misfortunes are truly small.

To sum up, when you face a big hardship, look upon this time with detached eyes, knowing that this is when your inner diamond is being polished the most, and when a smaller hardship emerges, look upon it as a simple problem to solve. I hope you won't give up. I hope you'll continue to persevere through your hardships, knowing that the journey of realizing your right will is itself a part of your soul training.

# III.

# *The* Art *of* Building Mental Strength

# 7. Deepening Your Understanding of Difficult Subjects

**QUESTION**

What can I do to develop a
better understanding of topics that
I have difficulty with,
such as politics and economics?

# ANSWER

### *"Begin by developing your interest in the subject."*

If you want to deepen your understanding of a difficult subject, such as politics or economics, you'll need to begin by developing your interest in the subject. A strong interest in a topic will help you find and gather the information you need from an array of sources, such as television, radio, newspaper, and other forms of media. If political and economic issues are the areas you want to learn more about, simply watching the news can teach you a great deal about them.

So if you're aiming for more than a slight understanding and want to form your own educated perspectives, you'll need to do more than just develop an interest in it. You'll need to build a deeper knowledge base on this topic, meaning, you'll need to study this subject in some depth. A solid knowledge base will help you form views that won't falter in the face of other people's differing opinions.

> *"A solid knowledge base will help you form views that won't falter in the face of other people's differing opinions."*

So, how much knowledge do you need in order to achieve this? This is a difficult question to answer, but in the end, the bottom line on average, I would say, is to read a thousand informative books about your subject. The knowledge of a thousand informative books on politics and economics will allow you to identify the errors and lies that journalists and news media are reporting. More than a thousand is even better, if you are capable of it.

But reading a thousand books may be more than most modern people with busy lives are capable of, and if this is the case for you, you don't necessarily need to read that many. You can focus most of your time on the subjects that are most important to you. I recommend dedicating 80 percent of your energy to your field of expertise and the remaining 20 percent to the subjects that you like the least. This will allow you to steadily build your knowledge base, little by little.

> *"The knowledge in a hundred books*
> *will allow you to develop*
> *your own opinions."*

The knowledge of one thousand books will be enough to distinguish between what's fact and fiction in the news media, but the knowledge of one hundred books will be enough to discuss the subject on a semi-expert level. If a hundred books is more than you are capable of reading immediately, you can set up a plan to read ten books a year, so that by the end of ten years, you'll have read a hundred. If you're capable of finishing twenty books every year, then you'll reach your goal by the end of five years. In this way, you can effectively make your goal more attainable by creating plans.

If international issues are an area you're particularly weak in, I recommend resolving to read a hundred books on this topic to steadily build your knowledge base. If your topic is specific, I think that a hundred books should be a reasonable goal. The constant race against time in our modern lives may make this a challenging goal, but it's definitely attainable if you look for small pockets of time to read throughout your daily life. If you continue to strive toward your goal in this way, I'm sure that doors will open for you.

The knowledge in a hundred books will allow you to develop your own opinions on the subject. What's more, you'll gradually see your understanding deepening over the course of your journey toward your goal.

One word of caution I want to leave you with, however, is the importance of waiting to express a lot of your opinion until you have reached a level of a true expert, even if you've become knowledgeable about it. If you're new to the subject, it's important to express opinions that stay true to the depth of your understanding and that refrains from being careless with your ideas.

Happy Science has published more than two thousand books of Truths that cover a wide range of subjects. The culture and knowledge you'll gain from reading one hundred Happy Science books are equivalent to reading ten thousand other informative books.

> *"It's also valuable to receive
> the help of knowledgeable friends."*

Consulting a friend is another way to learn about areas that lie outside your expertise. An intelligent person should be able to explain what something means and whether someone's opinion is really correct. Learning from others allows you to understand difficult topics in the course of several minutes, when you may have needed ten years to study and comprehend them by yourself. Sometimes, just a single explanation from someone is all that's necessary.

To attract intelligent friends, it helps to be a good person. The key is to be the kind of person an intelligent person would want to spend time with. There are an infinite number of people in the world to meet, many of whom are very intelligent and could give you answers to questions that would have taken you ten years to arrive at on your own.

Identifying who these intelligent people are may be challenging, so the important thing to do is to meet new people and stay in touch with people on a regular basis. Try to find out who is knowledgeable about what topics so you'll know who to contact when you encounter something that you don't understand.

Some of us, however, have no time at all to study a new subject, in which case, asking someone else to study the subject is yet another way. For example, if you wanted to learn more about the activities of the United Nations, you could ask a friend who's well-versed in this subject to read a book on it and explain it to you later. Of course, it's important to put your own effort into studying the subject, but it's also valuable to receive the help of knowledgeable friends.

# 8. Examining Our Inner Selves Spiritually

**QUESTION**

Can you give me advice on how to examine my inner self objectively?

> *"One important aspect is understanding the spiritual connection between our body and soul."*

One important aspect of examining our inner selves objectively is understanding the spiritual connection between our body and soul. If you could see through spiritual eyes, you would discover that your physical body houses a multiple-layered soul that looks identical to your physical body. In the outermost layer, the astral body, you'd find the functions of your spiritual heart and mind, as well as various other functions that are each associated with a different area of your physical body. Your soul is constructed of many integrated functions that are being directed as a whole.

For example, you'd find that your chest, not your head, is the main seat of your spiritual heart; your spiritual heart is found around the area of your physical heart. Our heart organs are very closely connected to the spiritual heart of our soul. Also, your head is the area where your mentality is found, while the will, for example, arises from around the chest, and emotions arise from the area of your liver. There's also the area of your belly and below, which is where the main source of your deep, fundamental energy lies. In the same way, there are other physical organs of your body that are mainly associated with various other spiritual functions.

Understanding this relationship is the basis of why Happy Science has been unsupportive of organ transplants from organ donors suffering from brain death. We know that our organs, including our hearts, possess a spiritual consciousness within them, so receiving a physical heart that originally belonged to someone else is almost akin to receiving the donor's spiritual heart. And to the donor's dismay, he or she may need to set out for the afterlife almost without a spiritual heart. This knowledge helps us understand the dangers we risk when undergoing organ transplantation, even though modern medicine has made this medical practice widespread.

I often talk about my teachings on love, wisdom, self-reflection, and progress, which are vital principles for attaining happiness. And these four principles are associated with specific parts of your body. Your head mainly corresponds to the principles of wisdom and progress, because they require a lot of mental thought. And the chest is the area that mainly corresponds to the principles of love and self-reflection, because these require more heart-based thinking.

We often find that people have developed one function more than the other. People with advanced pragmatic skills are often found to have developed the area from the neck up, and people with spiritual leanings, such as Buddhist priests, are more developed from the neck down. For example, if you are a Buddhist priest, you're very advanced at practicing the principles of love and self-reflection but not as highly capable in the pragmatic areas of work. People with Buddhist-priest-like personalities have a richly cultivated heart in their soul.

*"Your soul is made up of many areas that are capable of thinking."*

Now that we understand the relationship between the body and the soul, we have a basis for discussing some key steps you can take to examine your inner self. Basically, we can say that the areas of your head and chest are the main parts of your spiritual body, and when we practice self-reflection, we often use the area of our head to reflect upon our heart. This is because we often need to use the mental aspects of our soul, such as our logic and intellect, to be able to examine the intentions and emotions that arise from within our heart, the main place where love and self-reflection are practiced. For example, when you reflect on relationship issues with your significant other, you're using your head to examine your spiritual heart and belly, the physical areas that such issues are mainly connected with. In other cases, it may be necessary to use the beautiful sensibilities of your heart to reflect on the thoughts that you've been contemplating in your mind. For example, when you feel ashamed of wrong thoughts, your heart is at work, encouraging you to self-reflect.

As you can see, your soul is made up of many areas that are capable of thinking, and one area can be used to examine another area. Each of the principles in the Fourfold Path—love, wisdom, self-reflection, and progress—corresponds to a different part of the soul. And if you have difficulty practicing one of the principles of the fourfold path, you can use the other three principles to examine and get to the root of the problem. For example, if you're having difficulty practicing love that gives to others, the root problem may be the insufficient use of wisdom to support your love. You can discover this root problem through your intellectual sense to examine how you've been practicing the principle of love.

Or, if you've been concentrating a lot on your self-reflection but this hasn't led to much progress, you may need to see it more from the perspective of progress. When you do, you may find that you haven't been truly reflecting, but looking for reasons or excuses for your issues. Looking at your self-reflection from the perspective of progress allows you to find the issues in your self-reflection.

> ## *"You'll begin to know which area is doing the thinking."*

Now, let's look in more detail at the relationship between the individual parts of the physical body and the Fourfold Path: the principle of love corresponds to the area of your chest, near your heart, and the principle of self-reflection to the lower abdomen. The principle of wisdom is more difficult to specify, since people's intelligence can vary. But a lot of your intellectual functions are carried out by the area of the back and side of your head. But those with less developed intelligence may be using the spiritual functions of the belly or heart to do more of their thinking.

Finally, the principle of progress corresponds to the forehead, where you'll find the frontal lobe. Yoga often talks about the chakra located between your eyebrows, which is the area of your body that emits your mental will. There are other areas on your body that let out the outward flow of your mental will, such as the palms of your hands, but you'll find the strongest will being emitted from the chakra on your forehead.

Practicing the principle of progress and controlling your willpower are very closely associated. It's difficult to achieve progress with a feeble willpower. Many people who haven't achieved much success are probably not directing enough willpower from their forehead. Very successful people usually possess very strong willpower and emanate strong energy from this area of their forehead.

When you become accustomed to examining your inner self and managing your soul, you'll begin to know which area is doing the thinking at the moment. And when your spiritual ability advances even further, you'll also begin to use all the different parts of your body to serve all the functions, such as your hands as your eyes to look at things, and your back as your ears to listen to sounds.

As I've said, our spiritual body is composed of separate parts with individual functions, but training will help you develop the ability to use different spiritual functions to perform the work of other areas, and you'll gain control of your soul to work according to your wishes. When you reach this state, having a physical body in this world will start to feel like a heavy burden on your soul. I hope that I've helped you to understand these mystical aspects of being a human and having a soul.

# 9. Dealing with Jealousy and Criticism

**QUESTION**

People at my new workplace are talking behind my back and accusing me of being overconfident. I'm just trying to be confident in myself and putting my best into my work, but I don't know how to tell who is right. What can I do to look at this situation objectively?

# ANSWER

## *"Pay attention to your peers to understand what they're thinking and doing."*

It's hard to tell whether or not your self-confidence is over-confidence when you are thinking only of yourself. Instead, I recommend paying attention to your peers to gain a better understanding of what they're thinking and doing. This will help you objectively understand how other people perceive you.

There is a simple way of recognizing when your self-confidence has become exaggerated. The telltale signs is when people speak ill of you and talk about you behind your back. People don't normally treat someone else this way unless they feel that this person is acting overly self-confidently, so this is a useful sign to look to as a yardstick.

Some degree of self-assertiveness is a natural part of being human, and when we use it to fulfill good intentions, it helps guide our growth and development. We humans definitely need an inner drive for self-improvement; otherwise we might stop growing. But sometimes, as we strive to improve, we breed discord between ourselves and others, which is why harmonizing principles are also necessary. And one of these harmonizing principles is the role that other people's emotions play in our relationships.

*"Jealousy can play a preventive role against excessive arrogance."*

I've only rarely talked about the human emotion of jealousy in a positive light when I teach the Truths. But jealousy sometimes plays a beneficial role in our lives. And one way it can do that is by curbing excessive self-assertiveness. When someone's desire to stand out becomes too strong, people around them start pulling them back into their true place, and that's how jealousy can be beneficial.

Imagine a successful woman who deserves her success for her outstanding character and the hard work she has put into her work. People who speak ill of her are bound to see their act of unkindness eventually reflecting upon themselves, while this successful woman will carry on normally, unfazed and unwounded. Or think of the hardworking, successful businessman who's earned the high esteem of his peers and enough wealth to build a splendid house. If he becomes the target of people's jealousy, their ill will is only going to reflect back upon themselves.

In contrast, someone with an exaggerated sense of self-importance, who hasn't put in the same kind of effort to achieve his success, will probably be suspected of having achieved his wealth and success dishonestly. Other people's criticism will greatly impact his conscience and will serve as a guardrail against him going further down the path of wrongdoing. In this way, jealousy can play a preventive role against excessive arrogance and can function as a harmonizing agent.

Jealousy can also play a positive role in our relationships with our life partners. Many men can probably relate to the difficulty of dealing with their wives' jealousy, but her jealousy may be the vital glue that's holding their marital relationship together. If wives gave their husbands complete freedom to do as they pleased, many marriages would probably be destroyed. When wives want to know what time their husbands are coming home and what they're planning to do over the weekend, a healthy form of jealousy is working to protect marital harmony and the welfare of the family.

Of course, I'm in no way justifying wrong forms of jealousy, but I would like to mention that becoming overly jealous and obsessive can give rise to marital discord in the end. There are always two sides to everything, and keeping this in mind can be helpful for dealing with jealousy.

> *"Calmly accept criticisms while you continue to develop your capabilities."*

As I've just explained, the voices of the people around you are the main way to diagnose an overconfident ego. But, there is also a less frequent situation, one that makes up about 10 percent of all cases, in which the criticism you receive is truly undeserved. In these cases, criticism is undeserved because the aspirations you've set for yourself are extremely high. The ideal that you're striving to attain is so great in scope or scale that the people around you have never imagined anything like it and so are unable to understand your words and actions, no matter how earnestly you persevere in your efforts to realize your goals. Therefore, they think you're just being overconfident.

If this is your situation, you'll need to be patient and endure this time of difficulty. Times like these that require perseverance are meant to appear throughout your life's journey. These difficult times are a call for you to bide your time patiently. Refrain from striking back at your critics by criticizing them. Instead, do your best to calmly accept their criticisms while you continue to develop your capabilities.

If the criticisms you're receiving are truly undeserved, they'll eventually fall away, and there will come a time when you'll know for certain whether your thoughts and actions were right. Until that time arrives, you must continue building and polishing your strengths, for if you don't, these criticisms may turn into truths. This is why it's important to persevere in this time of difficulty. If you believe that the scope of your aspirations is truly great, then make this time of adversity a time of perseverance and hone your capabilities steadfastly.

# CHAPTER TWO

# *How to Become an* Influential Leader

# I.

# *The* Art *of*
# Surviving *in*
# *a* Tough World

# 10. The Source of Leadership

QUESTION

It's often said that it takes wisdom
and courage to lead others.
But how can I acquire wisdom
and courage?

## ANSWER

## "Acquiring wisdom is one of life's greatest purposes."

We have many purposes in life, and one of them is to gain wisdom. Wisdom is something we can take back with us when we eventually return to the other world after several decades of life in this world. The purpose of our spiritual training here is to gain wisdom, and the way we gain wisdom is by assiduously learning different things and accumulating various experiences. We can't acquire wisdom and make it our own unless we go through these experiences ourselves. We can rarely gain wisdom only through reading. It's only by putting into practice what we've learned from books and studies and going through a process of trial and error that we come to know how to live a truly splendid and authentic life. To gain such wisdom is one of the purposes of life.

There is something deep and exquisitely profound about the word *wisdom*. Put simply, when we attain a certain level of wisdom, we will become a god—a divine spirit, or a high spirit—in the afterworld. This is the magnitude of gaining wisdom. Those who acquire wisdom become gods because they can teach a wide array of people.

Even if we pursue wisdom unceasingly and diligently, it's still hard to come by. So we need to keep trying one thing after another for years. We become leaders when we're able to teach many people and offer them ways of life and perspectives that guide them to the right path. And when our souls become abundant with wisdom, we can join the ranks of the gods.

The wisdom we gain is of great worth. When we leave this world, we have to leave behind everything that pertains to the physical body. We can't take back with us the food we consume, the money we earn, the titles we hold, the companies we work for, or the buildings and land we own. But we *can* take wisdom back with us.

I often say that the only things you can take with you to the afterlife are your heart and your mind. But what really matters is the wisdom you've accumulated within yourself. Whether you triumph in this lifetime depends on the quality and quantity of wisdom you cultivate throughout the course of your life. In this sense, acquiring wisdom is one of life's greatest purposes.

# "Wisdom is what gives courage a clear direction to follow."

Courage is the zeal, or the driving force, behind action, but courage can push forward our action in a clear direction only when coupled with wisdom. Courageous acts without wisdom often end in failure. When courage is not accompanied by wisdom, it often mutates into a brute strength that destroys not only yourself, but also many others around you. In this sense, decisions made without wisdom are often very risky.

Some may think that taking any action is better than taking no action at all, but this is not true. Success comes to us only when we use wisdom to guide and drive our actions forward. Courage is like a burning energy that pushes us forward but needs to be channeled in the right direction. And wisdom is what gives courage a clear direction to follow.

The topic of wisdom and courage reminds me of Manjushri, the bodhisattva who represents wisdom and courage.* In statues,

---

* Manjushri was a disciple of Shakyamuni Buddha who, two to three hundred years after Shakyamuni's death, spread the Buddha's teachings in southern India. Manjushri's activities became the source of the Mahayana movement in Buddhism.

Manjushri holds in one of his hands what is known as "Manjushri's sharp sword of wisdom." Manjushri's sword represents the power of wisdom to cut through all worldly attachments and physical illusions. In this way, wisdom can be likened to a sword.

Courage is the power that drives us forward, and wisdom is what channels courage in the right direction. But keeping a good balance between wisdom and courage can be quite a challenge. If we place too much emphasis on accumulating wisdom, we may lessen our incentive to take action, so we should be careful not to spend all our time in deep thought.

To acquire wisdom, we need to gain both knowledge and experience, as well as to cultivate and refine our character. It's also equally important that we learn from the wisdom of many other people.

> *"Wisdom and courage are essential for the realization of justice."*

When we integrate wisdom into courage and put them into practice together, they manifest as justice. Justice is whatever action brings about the greatest happiness for the greatest number of people and contributes to the happiness of all people. Wisdom is what makes justice truly just. If our actions aren't backed by wisdom, they can easily turn into mere disruption, just as some agitators and revolutionary groups do nothing more than disturb the peace of society. For example, activists who become violent in protests may seem energetic and fearless. But their actions are not recognized as righteous acts if they don't contribute to the happiness of the whole society. Activists need the wisdom to know whether their actions are truly promoting the good.

The same holds true for religion. I believe that all religious groups engage in their activities with a courageous spirit. But what's important is that they have a solid basis of wisdom that will tell them what will bring the greatest happiness to the greatest number of people. They must always consider what will bring the most good to people today as well as to future generations as they write a new history. Wisdom and courage are essential for the realization of justice. And the fruit of justice is public happiness—the happiness of the many.

> *"Set aside quiet time to look within and refine your inner self while at the same time fulfilling your public role to bring about justice."*

Because justice often leads to public happiness, if you are only concerned about your own personal happiness, you may have little room for realizing justice. If all you wish is to achieve personal happiness, or happiness for yourself, you could perhaps find it by secluding yourself in a mountain. You may find your life quite comfortable and pleasant if you can free yourself from all the troubles and difficulties that are bothering you now. But you may have to resist that temptation if you want to contribute to public happiness, or the happiness of the many. There are times when you have to take courage to blaze a trail for the many who are lost and suffering on their paths to happiness.

Wisdom and courage are essential to bringing about public happiness, which naturally leads to the manifestation of justice. But in the process of realizing justice, we may find ourselves amid conflicts. And this is when we face the challenge of maintaining a balance between our personal happiness or peace of mind and public happiness, the happiness of the whole society. If we aim to achieve both our personal happiness and public happiness—to pursue our own enlightenment while also using courage to promote justice—we must regularly set aside quiet time to look within and refine our inner self while at the same time fulfilling our public role to bring about justice.

In my case, I often meditate and communicate with divine spirits in heaven. But if this were all I did, I wouldn't have an opportunity to share with the public the things that my enlightenment has allowed me to find and discover. This is why I give public talks. This often becomes a spiritual battle that I have to fight, because some people in my audience bring along evil spirits with them. As I talk in front of the audience, I use the swords and arrows of my will to fight these negative spirits. This is a very real battle that I often have to fight.

> *"One goal is to achieve peace of mind by harmonizing the mind, and the other is to contribute to the happiness of many people."*

Let me briefly summarize what I've said so far. Wisdom gives direction to courage and brings about justice as a result. The realization of justice would lead to the happiness of the many, or public happiness, which is one of the goals that we Happy Science aim to achieve. However, as we pursue this goal, the issue of balancing personal happiness and public happiness comes into play.

As long as we are only pursuing our own happiness, we don't think about realizing justice and public happiness. So we should consciously hold onto a wish to bring happiness to all people and make the effort to spread public happiness. But when we focus on realizing happiness for the many, we may find ourselves losing the energy we need to achieve individual happiness. So, it's important to take the time to study and enlighten yourself, and then when you set foot outside, switch gears and work for the happiness of the many.

Buddhism teaches to seek enlightenment above and save people below. This means that while we should aspire to reach the infinite heights of enlightenment, we should, at the same time, do all we can to bring salvation to as many people as possible. These two goals point in different directions, and religion constantly aims to achieve both of them. One goal is to achieve peace of mind by harmonizing the mind, and the other is to contribute to the happiness of many people. This dichotomy may cause us to sway from one side to the other, but we should still strive to achieve both goals. And that is why wisdom and courage are essential to achieving both of them.

# 11. The Principle of Market Survival

## QUESTION

I work for a home appliance manufacturer, and our business is easily affected by economic conditions. How can we, as employees, maintain a richness of mind even during bad economic times and overcome the hardships our company faces?

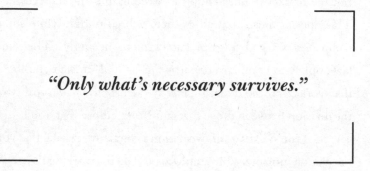

*"Only what's necessary survives."*

My answer to this question will vary depending on the position and responsibility you hold in the company, that is,
whether you're a CEO, a senior executive, a department manager,
or a rank-and-file employee.

There may be little we can do as individuals when the trends
of the times and the direction our country is heading are against
us. At times like these, business owners and executives suffer because their ideas alone are not enough to pull their companies
out of a slump. It becomes especially challenging when there is a
social trend that affects business, such as an economic downturn
or deflation. But no matter what situation we find ourselves in,
there is only one thing that we must do, and that is live faithfully
according to the principle that only what's necessary survives.

There are many electronics manufacturers out there, and it

can be hard to tell which ones are needed and which ones aren't. But the market is unrelenting in weeding out the unnecessary. This doesn't mean that all of them will go under: while some companies will go bankrupt, surely some will survive. The same law applies to company departments as well as each employee that works in these departments. We all face the harsh reality of the division between those that survive and those that don't.

So if you'd like to survive within a company, it's vital that you become an indispensable employee and do the work that's necessary to the company. And your company's survival in the market depends on whether there's a demand for your company.

> *"The first step you should take is to lower unit prices by reducing costs as much as possible."*

Goods and services that sell like hotcakes during an economic boom stop selling as soon as a recession hits. What do you think you should do when your customers stop buying your products?

The first step you should take is to lower unit prices by reducing costs as much as possible. When people face salary cuts and loss of income, they only have two purchasing options: they can either buy a less expensive product or buy the product that's the best value. They may even stop purchasing anything altogether. To cope with this situation, you need to lower prices, and to do this, you need to reduce the costs of producing your goods and services.

There must be things you can do to cut costs. Review your management procedures to find out if there are any areas where you've been lax and then improve those areas so you can get the highest productivity out of the lowest number of employees possible. Reduce expenses as much as possible by eliminating defective products and decreasing waste, excess stock, and unnecessary parts. You have to be strict in the management of your business.

*"Why would your customers need to purchase your products and services?"*

Another step you need to take is to consider why your customers would find your products and services necessary. Why would your customers need to purchase your products and services? You need to answer this question.

When the economy was good, your customers may have purchased your product simply because they had the money to spend. All you had to do was show them that it was within their budget. But during bad economic times, when you're not sure how much they're willing to spend or whether they have any money to spare for your product, you first have to show them how your product or service fills a need. Making them realize that they need your product adds value to your product. The key is to find out why your consumers should want your product and then offer what they need. This is the only way to survive in a tough market.

> *"Always maintain a peaceful mind,*
> *no matter how difficult the situation*
> *you find yourself in may be."*

When the economy goes into recession, I give more lectures on the topic of business and management because there is an increasing demand for them. And when people have tried all the methods and approaches but still find themselves unable to generate much profit, I start speaking on the topic of how to maintain peace of mind during hard times.

If you find yourself struggling to make a profit, the least you can do is maintain a calm mind. In times of financial despair, engaging in contention and conflict would only make you miserable. Just as a samurai puts on a brave display even in times of adversity, always maintain a peaceful mind, no matter how difficult the situation you find yourself in may be.

*"As long as we keep making the necessary effort, the path will open before us."*

When the economy was good, the consumer electronics industry and other industries alike enjoyed profitable sales without much effort. In particular, the home electronics industry in Japan grew dramatically following the end of World War II. But even businesses in the most thriving industries eventually hit a plateau and faced a shakeout in which companies were eliminated or acquired through competition.

Take, for example, the automotive industry in Japan. Even during the recession in the 1990s, some auto manufacturers continued to do well, and their competitors may have felt jealous of their successes. But even these successful companies faced a battle for survival, because there are limits to the number of people who drive and to available road space. To survive this market curtailment, these auto companies have been striving to distinguish themselves from their competitors. Frankly, this is the only way to stay in business in a competitive market.

In the long run, it benefits the greater part of society when the companies that meet their customers' demands survive. However tough the reality may be, only companies that become indispensable to society can survive in the market, and only employees that are indispensible to their companies can survive in the corporate world. As long as we keep making the necessary effort, the path will open before us.

*"Keep thinking about what it is that people need, desire, and value."*

It's only natural for things that are useless or harmful to eventually be discarded. Strange though it may be, religions and businesses are both subject to the same sifting process. I have said that religious groups will also face a shakeout that will separate beneficial ones from harmful ones, and the religious world as a whole will not improve until the misguided ones are expelled altogether. In fact, more than a few Japanese religious groups that were founded at about the same time as I founded Happy Science in 1986 have fallen apart, although the mass media at that time ranked these groups with Happy Science. I believe that society eventually made a decision not to grant these unwanted or harmful religious groups protection and tax privileges under the religious corporation law.

The same principle that applies to for-profit companies applies to religious groups. Religions are no exception to this rule, and they aren't allowed to do everything their own way. There are both good religions and bad religions, and the ones that are harmful to society will perish. Whether it be religion or anything else, things that people neither desire nor need sooner or later come to an end.

This shakeout principle applies to everything from businesses to religions. And to survive it, we need to keep thinking about what it is that people need, desire, and value and strive to make improvements year in and year out. We simply can't expect to survive by doing the same old thing.

# 12. The Makings of Legendary Figures

**QUESTION**

How can I become a greathearted and influential figure like the legendary Japanese samurais Ryoma Sakamoto and Takamori Saigo?

# ANSWER

> ## *"What makes people rise to greatness is not necessarily their latent talent, but rather their diligent effort."*

It is true that both Ryoma Sakamoto and Takamori Saigo* became great figures in history because their souls were endowed with the aptitude to accomplish great feats. But it is not the innate qualities that make someone great. Even those who are born with ample talent may not be able to achieve great success. Conversely, there are those who may have seemed to lack aptitude but still, through hard work, made a name for themselves in the world. What makes people rise to greatness is not necessarily their latent talent, but rather their diligent effort.

To join the ranks of the great figures in history, you have to work a hundred times harder than the average person. And to do this, you need to develop your greatest strengths to the maxi-

---

* Ryoma Sakamoto (1835–1867) and Takamori Saigo (1827–1877) were both leaders of the Meiji Restoration movement, which peacefully restored power to the emperor from the Tokugawa shogunate and ushered in a new era of modernization and prosperity in Japan.

mum extent. This is an essential practice for achieving greatness, whether you run your own business or work for a company. No matter what field of expertise you pursue, you have to keep making the effort to cultivate your strengths until you can say with confidence that you are clearly and surely helping and benefiting others.

Once you've made a name for yourself in a certain field, you can extend your reach to other fields. The first step to achieving greatness is to attain a certain degree of accomplishment in your primary field of expertise, because without this, you will have a hard time getting people to recognize you for your efforts in any other fields.

> *"Train and polish your skills until you become one of the best in the field."*

Not many people know that Ryoma Sakamoto first became famous by mastering swordsmanship. He gained nationwide fame at a young age for achieving the rank of acting master of swordsmanship at the dojo of Master Sadakichi Chiba. In fact, many of the great Japanese figures at that time, including Kaishu Katsu and Takayoshi Kido, mastered swordsmanship because it was the "weapon" they needed to go out into the world and gain influence. So they labored long and hard to master this skill. All these legendary Japanese heroes—Sakamoto, Katsu, and Kido alike—trained day in and day out to practice their swordsmanship.

There were other skills that they could have mastered at that time, and one of them was the study of Western sciences. Similarly, there are a variety of "weapons" you can use to go out into the world. So discover your own weapon, and train and polish your skills to use your weapon until you become one of the best in that field. You'll then be able to develop your expertise in other fields and grow into a person of great influence.

> *"Laying a solid foundation in one field will make it much easier for you to master other fields."*

In the early stages of the Happy Science movement, I published a series of spiritual messages I received from the high spirits in heaven. I decided to do this even though it would have been sufficient simply to publish my own ideas to expound on my teachings of the Truths. The reason I did this was because I thought that the starting point of my activities should be to convey that the spirit world really does exist. And to do this, I wanted to show that each and every spirit had a unique, individual personality.

No matter what you do, you need to lay a firm foundation in one area before moving on to other fields. If you neglect to take this approach and try to do everything all at once, it will be difficult for you to achieve great success even if you're gifted. So I suggest that you focus on one area and develop your expertise in that area first. Laying a solid foundation in one field will make it much easier for you to master other fields.

You have to practice asceticism in the sense that you have to focus on one field and give up all others until you achieve the results you want in that field. Without this attitude, you'll have difficulty succeeding in even one area.

The first step to great success is to build a firm foundation in one area, become one of the best in the field, and reach a level that others can't easily achieve. I hope you'll keep this in mind as you continue your efforts to achieve your goal.

# II.

# *The* Art *of* Gaining Trust

# 13. The Difference between Love and Ego

**QUESTION**

What should I be especially careful about
when I'm working with others,
particularly associates and
people I supervise?

## "We should be benefitting both the company and the people who work under us."

At work, it's quite natural that people in higher positions should tell their subordinates what to do, and they often need cooperation and help from their associates to get their work done. When they assign or delegate tasks to others, managers expect a certain level of performance from their subordinates and associates. They give them orders and make requests so they can get the job done with the expected results.

One thing that managers need to be careful about is not to become egoistic when they're working with others. When we're in a leadership position, we should be benefitting both the company and the people who work under us. We shouldn't give orders and make requests with the intention of taking all the credit for the job. But in reality, many people take all the credit for results they've achieved through the support and help of their assistants and colleagues.

*"Discern whether you're doing it from love as a leader or from an egoistic desire to achieve your own goals."*

It is important that those in higher positions, whether managers or mentors, lead the people under them. Without the guidance of those with a higher perspective, their subordinates would not know what to do. For example, even if an entry-level employee has the potential to eventually become a company president, the employee won't be able to do the work of a manager or director from the first day on the job. Those in leadership positions need to give new employees direction to follow.

When you lead others, it is important to clearly discern whether you're doing it from love as a leader or from an egoistic desire to achieve your own goals. There is nothing wrong with giving instructions to others as long as you're doing it with a leader's love, because that means you're doing it out of a desire to guide others' growth. However, it's not right to tell others what to do if your motivation is to manipulate them for your own benefit.

The difference between a leader's love and selfish desire lies in the motive behind the action. Are your actions coming from a sincere wish to help someone become a better person? Or are they motivated by a desire to benefit yourself and an intention to take all the credit for yourself? The answer to this question reveals your true motive.

> "The difference between a leader's love and selfish desire lies in the motive behind the action."

Imagine that you've asked an acquaintance to help you with a particular task. It's not right to just give him instructions without considering how he might benefit, and it's not right to claim all the credit and feel pleased with yourself for completing the task. On the other hand, if your acquaintance can gain something valuable and contribute to the well-being of many other people by working for you, then you're on the right track and your leadership is an act of love.

You need to make a clear distinction between the two cases: whether you're guiding others to grow out of a love of leadership or taking advantage of them for your own personal benefit. To know which one describes you, you need to constantly ask yourself if you're working solely for yourself or if you're taking into consideration what will benefit other people. After examining your motive, if you can say that your actions are based on love, then you can fully commit yourself to your work and not hesitate to give orders and instructions to your subordinates and associates so you can get the job done.

# 14. How to Effectively Give Reprimands

**QUESTION**

What is the most effective way to
reprimand my subordinates at work,
when it's essential to do so?

## ANSWER

*"You'll need to do it with a heart of love and choose the best approach for each person."*

Your question isn't about the nature of a reprimand, but rather about the technique, and that's a matter of the leader's skill. When you're in a managerial position, you can't afford to tell your staff, "Don't worry about making mistakes. I'll take care of whatever mistakes you make." If you manage people with this kind of attitude, you're not only asking for trouble, but also failing to fulfill your responsibility as a manager. You'll inevitably face situations that force you to reprimand your subordinates. But when you do so, you'll need to do it with a heart of love and choose the best approach for each person.

First, let's consider how to reprimand competent people. When reprimanding competent people, you'll need to discern whether they have a lot of pride in their capabilities or if they are more of a carefree type. You don't want to admonish those who take pride in themselves in front of other people. You can deeply hurt their most essential identity if you give them a stern reprimand in front of others, and you'll end up losing the cooperation and support that you could have relied on from them. You need to be particularly careful when you have to reprimand male subordinates who take a lot of pride in themselves. You'd never want to scold them in front of women. Proud men suffer most excruciating emotional damage when women speak about them behind their backs. They may be able to bear receiving reprimands in front of other men, but scolding them in front of women will irreversibly hurt their pride, arousing a feeling of animosity against you.

When you have to reprimand those with a lot of pride, I suggest that you do so in private. These people need special care. Talk to them in a separate room or talk over coffee or lunch, for example. This is how you can avoid making enemies of them and guide them toward a better direction while maintaining their support.

On the other hand, you can reprimand easygoing and carefree people in front of others. These people like to be in the limelight, so they don't mind being scolded loudly and out in front of everyone. Receiving a severe rebuke seems almost unreal to them, so their feelings don't get hurt that much. Reprimanding this type of person in private usually has little effect.

## *"First discern whether they're the carefree type or the sensitive type."*

The two legendary Japanese professional baseball players—Sadaharu Oh and Shigeo Nagashima—represent the two types of people I've just described. Tetsuharu Kawakami, who was the manager of the Yomiuri Giants at the time that both of these players played for the team, understood the difference between them.* Kawakami would always reprove Oh, who was the former type, behind closed doors in private, and scold Nagashima, who was the latter type, in front of many other players.

Nagashima was a star player who represented the team. So when Kawakami yelled at him in front of everyone, his teammates saw him as a scapegoat for the whole team and were inspired to train harder. As a result, the whole team's morale improved. Nagashima was a cheerful and carefree personality who never

---

* Sadaharu Oh holds the record for the most home runs ever hit (868), and Shigeo Nagashima is one of the most popular professional baseball players in the history of Japanese baseball. They both played for the Tokyo Yomiuri Giants in the Japanese Central League when Tetsuharu Kawakami, who himself was a legendary baseball player, served as a manager of the Giants. Kawakami led the team to nine consecutive championships with Oh and Nagashima dominating the batting titles during this period.

held a grudge over stern reprimands, so Kawakami could scold him without worrying too much about hurting his feelings. On the other hand, Kawakami never scolded Oh in front of others, because he knew that doing so would damage Oh's batting.

Scolding the Nagashima type in front of others can have a positive effect. So you don't need to hesitate; you can scold employees like him in a loud voice so that everyone else can hear you. Their coworkers will encourage them to do a better job next time, and that will help them grow and improve. One important thing to remember, when you reprimand this type, is to let go of what happened right away. By the next day, you should be acting as if you never scolded them.

As we've seen in this example, when you're reprimanding competent, capable people, first discern whether they're the carefree, Nagashima type or the sensitive, Oh type, and reprimand them in the appropriate manner depending on their type. Leaders who lack managerial skills often make the mistake of scolding the Oh type in public and the Nagashima type in private.

> *"What's essential is to give them tasks that are commensurate with their ability."*

You may also need to manage employees who seem to be incapable of doing their work, and you may secretly wish they'd be transferred to a different department. But in the business world, once they're assigned to your department, as their boss, you're responsible for the work they do, and it's usually not easy to send them off to another department.

When managing unskilled people, you need to determine the limits of their capabilities. Assigning them tasks that they're not capable of handling will only bring suffering to themselves and those around them. For example, if an employee lacks leadership skills but you assign her to a managerial post, it may lead to serious problems that bring misery to everyone, including her and people who work with her.

When you have incompetent people working under you, instead of giving up on them or treating them as a burden, consider which area or type of work they would perform best, and give them the amount of responsibility they can handle. Based on this assessment, you need to limit the types of tasks you assign them. Once you've clarified the range of their responsibilities and assigned them specific jobs that they can fulfill comfortably, you'll also need to keep reminding them to complete the tasks that you've given them.

It will do no good to take pity on their incompetence and feel bad for them. What's essential is to give them tasks that are commensurate with their ability. For example, if you have an elderly person working under you, you may feel bad and be tempted to assign an important task to this person. But, however cruel it may seem, if you have a younger person who is more capable of performing the task, you must assign that job to that person. This is simply what you, as their boss, must do.

> *"It's your duty as a supervisor or manager to be able to foresee precisely where your people are likely to fail."*

Competent people may feel frustrated and lose motivation if you keep sticking your nose in every detail. So you can entrust them and increasingly delegate more work to those who can handle it.

But you can't treat incompetent people the same way. You need to forewarn them of the mistakes they're likely to make and point out the possible risks of failure beforehand. Otherwise, you will end up reprimanding them forever for each of the mistakes they make, which would be emotionally unhealthy for both yourself and everyone who works under you.

So you, as their supervisor, must be able to foresee the holes that your subordinates may fall into, warn them, and give them a word of advice about how to handle the potential pitfalls when you assign them jobs. It's your duty as a supervisor or manager to be able to foresee precisely where your people are likely to fail. If your subordinates repeatedly make the same mistake because of your inability to predict possible failures, then the fault lies not with your subordinates, but with you.

So when you have people working under you, I suggest that you group them into these three different types: competent and prideful people, competent and carefree people, and incompetent people. Then guide the people in each group in the way that most suits them. Your ability to do this is a test of your leadership skills. At the same time, keep in mind that there are many more types of people in real life than the three I've discussed here. So I recommend that you adjust your treatment of each person accordingly. I hope that you will be able to discover and try out a variety of different ways to guide and lead many types of people.

# 15. The Limits of a Sympathetic Leader

**QUESTION**

What kind of love should leaders practice
to truly help others grow?

# ANSWER

## *"While pathos is a passive love, agape is an active love."*

We can categorize love into two types based on their essential nature. The first type of love is what I will call "pathos" for now. This is a sympathetic love. Unlike *eros*, which is central to romantic love, this is a love that instantaneously evokes self-sacrificing feelings of pity. This is an instant emotion of sympathetic love, based on pity. The other kind of love is called "agape." Agape is an intelligent love, and we sometimes refer to it as Hellenic love. These are the two types of love: pathos and agape.

Pathos is closer to the feeling of sympathy. The heart of feeling bad for others and lamenting their misfortunes is something that we should treasure. But if we get carried away by this emotion, we'll be doing nothing but consoling one another. You may be able to share a sense of unity based on this feeling, but you'll also find yourself constantly in the melancholy mood of a wake or funeral, which makes you feel as if you're not even allowed to smile.

On the other hand, agape, or love with wisdom, embodies a formula for expanding love. In other words, agape contains a creative aspect that has to do with spreading love. Agape is also a lofty and very spiritual love that lets us guide and lead others. In this sense, you could say that agape is the love of the angels or deities. Simply put, agape is love of those who have the power to save others.

While pathos is a passive love, agape is an active love. So it wouldn't be right to understand love simply as a feeling of sympathy, pity, or empathy.

> *"We can accomplish greater feats when we transform our personal love into a love that includes a vision of the future."*

Among Christians, there are many who limit themselves to practicing the love of pathos, believing that love is a sympathetic feeling for those who suffer. Of course, love that comforts others is essential when people feel weak or disheartened. It's natural to want to be held in someone's arms when we're hurting. But at the same time, we should know that the love that helps people grow is also essential. When you recognize both types of love, you'll be able to tell which type you're leaning toward now.

Let me illustrate this with the example of Takamori Saigo, a nineteenth-century Japanese samurai and legendary hero. Saigo was indeed a great figure in history who inspired and influenced many people. But he could have accomplished a greater feat if he had been able to acquire deeper wisdom. Saigo felt pity for the young, disaffected samurais who rebelled against the government, so he decided to stake his life for them. He showed his love by meeting their request to become the leader of the rebel army and by dying with the young samurais. Saigo was certainly a person of love, but his love was weighted toward sympathy and pity.

Why was Saigo unable to practice agape, love accompanied by high intellect, during his later years? It was because he wasn't aware of the changes taking place in the world. Some of the Japanese government officials had had a chance to visit and stay in the West for a couple of years at the beginning of the Meiji period, and they had seen clearly the direction that Japan needed to take. However, Saigo and other officials who hadn't traveled to the West and had stayed in Japan their entire lives couldn't understand this new vision of the future and were extremely concerned about what would happen to the samurais and warrior families of Japan. The government was split into two groups—those who had seen the West and those who hadn't—and it turned out that Japan moved in the direction of those who had seen a clear vision of their country's future by visiting the West.

Saigo died a tragic death because he didn't have a vision of the future. He did play a key role in bringing about a peaceful revolution during the Meiji Restoration. But after the new Meiji government was established, he didn't see which direction Japan should head toward. This is probably what brought an end to his mission and eventually led to his death.

We can accomplish greater feats when we transform our personal love into a love that includes a vision of the future. We need the kind of love that lets us see both our own future and the future of the people we help and lead.

> *"Love that contains wisdom can bring about fruitful results."*

When providing aid to developing countries that suffer from water shortages, some people may say that we should give them water, while others may say that we should teach them how to dig wells. If we choose to simply give them water, we'll be giving them water forever. But if we teach them how to dig wells, they'll be able to gain access to water by themselves. So it's better to provide agricultural and industrial skills and knowledge rather than simply giving them material aid.

There are many Christian organizations that take part in charity and volunteer activities to offer material aid to the victims of wars and disasters. I'm sure their activities are helping people in need. But we can practice a greater love when we guide them in a way that helps them get back on their feet and build a better society on their own.

Today, India faces a lot of problems, including poverty, disease, and violence, and the country is in a predicament. Volunteer activities such as those offered by Mother Teresa's Missionaries of Charity are not enough to truly save India on their own. What India truly needs to save itself from its present state are people who have a vision for the future of their country. India needs leaders who can see the right direction to lead their country in, like the Japanese leaders that successfully brought about the Meiji Restoration. If there are people in India who know why and how Japan achieved its growth, they can share their wisdom so that other people will also see the direction they need to take. This kind of love that contains wisdom can bring about fruitful results.

> *"The greater your wisdom, the greater
> your love will become."*

Wisdom is indispensable when we give love to others. When you give someone a helping hand, you need to see beyond the end of your nose. It takes great wisdom to save all of humankind. This is not an issue of whether love or wisdom comes first. We need *both* wisdom and love. The greater your wisdom, the greater your love will become. For your love to grow, it's imperative that you develop your wisdom.

If you want to supply a large amount of water, using a pail or basin won't serve your purpose. You need to show people how to lay water pipes so that they'll have running water. We need wisdom to support love. We need love to further develop wisdom. It's because we understand others' sufferings and troubles that we want to use our wisdom to help them solve their problems.

Both love and wisdom are essential to spreading our global activities of creating an ideal world on Earth. If you think that only a handful of people should work hard to turn this world into an ideal place, your love is still small. When you cultivate true love, you'll want a great number of people to join you so that to-gether you can save as many people as possible. Again, you need wisdom to achieve a greater love. I hope that you'll treasure love that contains wisdom and practice love that contains sympathy and kindness as you interact with the people around you.

# III.

# *The* Art *of* Leading *with* Love *and* Wisdom

# 16. Enlightenment and the Capacity of the Soul

**QUESTION**

Great figures are often described as highly enlightened and as having great spiritual capacity. What's the difference between these qualities?

ANSWER

> *"Those with a propensity to broaden their spiritual capacity have more potential to grow."*

Let's say that there are two people who have both achieved the state of bodhisattva.* This means that they've attained the same level of enlightenment and have the same level of awareness and understanding of the Truths. But that doesn't necessarily mean that they'd both be able to achieve the same results on any particular task. For example, one might be pursuing the heights of excellence strictly and narrowly while the other takes on a broad range of tasks profoundly and extensively. It's hard to say which type is better, but it seems that souls that have the propensity to broaden their possibilities have more potential in the long run.

Even though they stand at the same level of spiritual awareness right now, souls that are open to broader possibilities

---

* Bodhisattvas, also known as angels, are spirits that reside in the seventh dimension of heaven. Their hearts are filled with love toward others, and their deeds are acts of selfless service.

have the potential to grow and become greater leaders. On the other hand, souls that have a more specific, limited view are more likely to come up against a wall in the course of their development.

We're all going through our own spiritual training over the course of time. And at some point, we may come across people who stand at the same level of spiritual awareness as we do. But those with a propensity to broaden their spiritual capacity have more potential to grow as they move into the future.

Even if we were born in the same era and practiced the same spiritual discipline, our leadership abilities may differ depending on the range of the experiences we acquire. Let's say that the head monk at a monastery has attained the state of bodhisattva and a businessman who has trained and disciplined his soul while living through turbulent days in the modern world has also achieved the state of bodhisattva. Even though the two people are in the same spiritual state at a particular point in time, in the long run, we can presume there will be a big gap in their leadership capabilities. By broadening the range of our experiences, we can further develop our potential to grow in the future.

> *"We can achieve a certain level of overall success by increasing the breadth of our activities."*

Those who can accept various types of people have great spiritual capacity, and it is the breadth of the soul that will eventually determine the amount of work they can accomplish.

Kanzo Uchimura (1861–1930) was a Japanese Christian leader of the Non-Church Movement* who attained the spiritual state of a tathagata.† During his life, he was very strict with his disciples. He rarely took on disciples—he only had twenty or thirty during the course of his entire life. But they were all truly excellent people and the best of the best. In contrast, other religious leaders with the same level of enlightenment as Uchimura's took on and trained many disciples and built orders with large followings. You could say that this is a matter of personal style or

---

* The Non-Church Movement is a Japanese Christian movement founded in 1901 by Kanzo Uchimura who encouraged followers to study the Bible at home without belonging to any specific church.

† Tathagatas are spirits that reside in the eighth dimension of heaven. Tathagatas have attained a higher level of spirituality than bodhisattvas. They teach fundamental philosophies and ideas that become the basis of the creation of new civilizations and cultures.

preference, but I think that we can make more efficient use of our time and bring about more educational benefits when we receive and teach many disciples.

Moreover, even if you haven't achieved a high level of enlightenment, you can still develop great potential for the future by accumulating a variety of experiences and cultivating a capacity to accept a wide variety of people. The more people you meet, the more opportunities you'll have to give love. So, even if people haven't attained a very high level of enlightenment, if they can perform various types of jobs and tasks, then their lives are valuable and meaningful in their own way.

If you compare Buddhism and Christianity in terms of their overall level of enlightenment as religions, Buddhism is clearly on higher ground. However, Christianity has spread to a much wider range of people. Both as individuals and as an organization, we can achieve a certain level of overall success by increasing the breadth of our activities even if we don't reach the highest height.

# 17. Five Weapons for Achieving Great Accomplishments

**QUESTION**

In one of your books, you use the phrase, "from personal happiness to public happiness."* I'm afraid that if I pursue personal happiness, I may end up thinking only about my own gain. But when I try to be of service to the world, I tend to overwork and sacrifice my own happiness. How can I achieve both personal happiness and public happiness?

## ANSWER

"*The practice of giving love will naturally lead you toward the happiness of the many.*"

It seems that you don't yet have a full understanding of the phrase "from personal happiness to public happiness," so let me explain. Personal happiness is a feeling of bliss that continues from this world through to the next. This is the happiness of enlightenment. What, then, is the happiness of enlightenment? It's a happiness that comes from knowing your true self and understanding the purpose of the universe from the perspective of your true self. With this understanding comes the realization that life is a gift that is given to you, and this joy of the soul leads to changed actions. When you achieve this happiness, it automatically makes you want to help change the world for the better.

In this way, personal happiness and public happiness work in a cycle. So if you think of personal happiness as being about

---

* Ryuho Okawa, *Utopia Souzouron* ["Discussions on the Creation of Utopia"] (Tokyo: IRH Press, 1997).

protecting your own interests, then you're mistaken. On the contrary, as I teach at Happy Science, personal happiness is the opposite of self-preservation, and you'll never achieve personal happiness as long as you're trying to protect your own interest. You will attain personal happiness when you abandon your worldly attachments and practice giving love to others instead of taking love from others. And the practice of giving love will naturally lead you toward public happiness, which is a love that brings happiness to many people.

To sum up, personal happiness and public happiness are not two separate states, but go hand in hand. In fact, public happiness is an expansion of your personal happiness. This is the true meaning of the phrase "from personal happiness to public happiness."

> *"Courtesy, wisdom, sincerity, justice, and valor: the five weapons you can use in the battlefield of life."*

Many people, especially young people, may not have been able to acquire the "weapons" they need to serve the world. You may not like the sound of the word "weapons," but the weapons I'm about to describe are the tools you need to contribute to the world.

You'll need to forge certain weapons before going out into the battlefield of life. You will need to fight a battle—not the type that involves physical violence, but one that involves practicing the Truths to bring about a big movement that will change your country for the better. To contribute to this movement, we all need certain weapons to fight with. So you'll need to ask yourself, "What weapons can I use to fight this battle?"

In one of my books, I list five virtues that are required of a leader: courtesy, wisdom, sincerity, justice, and valor.* You can think of these five virtues as weapons you can use to serve the world.

The first virtue, courtesy, is a weapon you can use to win recognition in the world. Next is wisdom, which includes knowledge and experience. This is a powerful weapon, and particularly for students, it's one of the most essential weapons. Sincerity is a virtue that helps you win other people's trust. Sincerity will help you build networks and make friends, which will lead you to great success. Justice is a virtue you can acquire by learning what is right and discarding what is wrong. Developing a mindset of justice will equip you with another weapon you can use to accomplish a feat. The final virtue is valor, which is the courage

---

* Ryuho Okawa, *Jinsei No Oudou Wo Kataru* ["The Royal Road of Life"] (Tokyo: IRH Press, 1993).

and ability to take action. Unfortunately, valor alone will not make you a leader in the true sense. You will need to acquire the other virtues first. Only when you acquire valor in addition to the other virtues can you become a true leader. In less developed societies, we find many people who have achieved leadership positions only with valor, but valor alone doesn't make them true leaders.

Courtesy, wisdom, sincerity, justice, and valor: these are the five weapons you can use in the battlefield of life, so make them your own. Arming yourself with these virtues is not a selfish act at all, because it will help you serve others and lead you to contribute to the happiness of the many.

# 18. Three Criteria for Assessing Leadership

**QUESTION**

What are the criteria for measuring the accomplishments of the great historical figures who led their nations and people politically or militarily?

## ANSWER

Among the historic figures lauded as heroes, some lived in the spiritual state of bodhisattvas or tathagatas, while others lived with their minds attuned to hell. The destinations they returned to after death vary greatly. So let's consider the criteria for assessing the leadership qualities of political and military leaders.

# 1. SELFLESS ACTS OF ALTRUISM

The first criterion for assessing leadership is selflessness: are they using their position for their own benefit or for the benefit of others? In other words, we should examine whether their actions arise from self-interest or from unselfish motives.

Their state of mind may or may not become apparent to others, but in the eyes of heaven, it's obvious and can be assessed precisely. Regardless of their status in this world, even if they're the president or prime minister, this is the first point they'll be checked on. So, it's important that leaders strive to cultivate a selfless heart and think about the happiness of many people.

For example, one of the greatest traits of Abraham Lincoln was his fair and selfless spirit. He always treated everyone equally and was never self-serving. Moreover, he was completely devoid of hypocrisy and genuinely wished for the happiness of many from the depths of his heart. People like Lincoln, who truly enjoyed serving others and sincerely felt that doing so was his calling or the vocation he was born to fulfill, are the strongest of the leaders.

Those who perform altruistic acts because they want to be recognized for their contributions are not genuinely selfless but egoistic. Even if someone tried to be like Albert Schweitzer and went to Africa as a medical missionary, built hospitals, and treated many patients, if his motive was solely to win respect and recognition for himself, his life was in vain.

Florence Nightingale was heavily criticized for trying to make a name for herself through her activities, but in the long run, she inspired and influenced a lot of people because her motives were selfless, and this influence became a source of virtue for her. Other people can typically tell whether someone's motives are genuine or superficial. Even if they're fooled for a time, they'll eventually figure it out. In most cases, the true motives behind our actions become clear by the time of our death. And if they don't, then future generations will surely discern the truth.

So the first criterion for assessing leaders is selflessness— whether they're altruistic or egoistic, or whether they're dedicated to serving others or protecting their own self-interest. One of the reasons Napoleon Bonaparte became so popular among his people was that he loved them. When Napoleon returned from his exile on the island of Elba, he received an enthusiastic welcome with open arms from the people in Paris, because they could keenly feel the love in his heart. Of course, Napoleon had a number of flaws, but he fulfilled the first criterion because he had a strong wish to devote his life to the welfare of others. The same is true of Alexander the Great.

## 2. CONTRIBUTION TO THE CREATION OF A UTOPIAN SOCIETY

The second criterion for assessing leaders is the contribution they've made to the creation of an ideal society through their political and military actions. It's extremely difficult to assess this, and even historians may not be able to tell whether a leader actually contributed to making this world a better place. In the end, all we can do is examine their actions over a long period of history.

Let's consider the actions of Abraham Lincoln as an example. During the American Civil War, people in the South spoke of Lincoln as if he were a devil. The movie *Gone with the Wind* depicts the anger and grudge of the South. This drama portrays the life of a dynamic woman in the South during a time when the "cruel" Union trampled on the Southern land and "murdered" the people. I was moved by the movie the first time I saw it, but when I watched it again later, after my spiritual awakening to the Truths, I no longer felt touched, because I could clearly discern the level of the writer's consciousness.

One of the issues with this movie is the way the heroine, Scarlet O'Hara, lived. To put it quite bluntly, I have to say that she led a pretty hellish life. The writer of this story used her artistry to depict the sublimity of the heroine's life, but anyone who leads the kind of life she led will likely end up in hell. From a spiritual point of view, the way she lives in the story is quite wretched, even though from a literary perspective, the book is acclaimed as a highly artistic work.

Another issue with the story is that the writer had an incorrect take on the nature of the Civil War. From a broader point of view, the Civil War was a collision between two conflicting values. At that time, people in the South used slaves as cheap labor to grow cotton. To them, the emancipation of slaves meant severe damage to their businesses. They fought the war to protect their economic interests. We need to compare the benefits of the Southern cause with the benefits of the Northern cause, which was to liberate the slaves, and assess which side held higher overall values based on the Truths.

Robert E. Lee, the legendary general of the Confederate Army during the Civil War, was a virtuous and well-respected man. After the war, he avoided being sentenced to death, became the president of Washington College (today, Washington and Lee

University), and remained in this position until his death. Lee was among the many people in the South who had considerable insight. However, Lincoln saw the world from an even higher perspective.

Lincoln thought about the future of America. He realized that if some states allowed people to keep slaves while others prohibited the practice, the country would be torn apart. Furthermore, he knew that accepting slavery and acknowledging that one race was superior to another would lead the nation to face serious problems in the future. He decided that slavery would be a great detriment to the future of America and carried out the Civil War with strong determination.

Contributing to the creation of an ideal world is the second criterion for assessing leadership quality. And to measure this quality, we first need to examine the leader's value judgments.

# 3. SPIRITUAL LEGACY

The third criterion for assessing leadership quality is the spiritual heritage a leader hands down to future generations. When we use this standard to compare Hitler with other leaders such as Napoleon and Alexander the Great, the difference becomes clear. As leaders, they may share some similarities, but they're certainly different on this point.

The mentalities of Alexander and Napoleon have been passed down as the spirits of their times and have influenced and inspired the generations that followed. Likewise, Lincoln's philosophy of human equality became the source of America's prosperity from the latter half of the nineteenth century into the twentieth century. America's prosperity was built by each one of the people who came from all over the world in pursuit of their dreams. And I think that Lincoln's philosophy that all human beings are equal was at the root of the nation's prosperity.

*"The biggest factor in assessing our leadership capability is the goal we aim to achieve."*

The overall capabilities of political and military leaders are assessed based on these three criteria. They don't receive a simple "pass or fail," but rather a grade for each criterion. And they are assessed based on the overall grade they achieve throughout the course of their lives.

Some people do well for the first half of their lives and start going down the wrong path in the second half. For example, not all the famous Japanese military leaders during the Sengoku period (from the middle of the fifteenth century to the end of the sixteenth century) returned to heaven after death. Shingen Takeda and Kenshin Uesugi both returned to the world of angels and divine spirits in heaven. But another famous warrior, Nobunaga Oda, was not able to return directly to heaven after death. Let's consider how Nobunaga differed from the first two leaders.

With respect to the third criterion, both Shingen and Kenshin handed down certain spiritual climates to later generations, and that's why they're still widely loved, long after their deaths. On the other hand, Nobunaga continued to be haunted by animosity. Nobunaga also seems to differ greatly from these two leaders with respect to the first criterion, altruistic or egoistic motives.

We probably can't get perfect scores on all three criteria, but the biggest factor in assessing our leadership capability is the goal we aim to achieve. It's not always the angels that gain political or military control, and you may wonder why this happens. But it's often hard to tell what it really means at the time, because it could be part of heaven's great plan.

# 19. Insight into the Future Situation of the World

**QUESTION**

Presently, it seems that the world is becoming a unipolar, U.S.-dominated world and that Christian values are becoming more prevalent. Under this circumstance, what are your visions or expectations for the future?

ANSWER

> ## *"Predicting negative events doesn't lead to positive outcomes."*

Back in 1990 and 1991, I used to listen to and accept the opinions of many different spirits in the spirit world. At that time, I incorporated the ideas of spirits in the Islamic world as well as Buddhist and Christian spirits. I also took in the opinions of spirits that specialized in prophecy, most of which belonged to the world of Rear Heaven.* But beginning around 1994, I started putting together the fundamental teachings for my organization, Happy Science, mainly based on the teachings of Shakyamuni Buddha, and began to clean out some of the ideas that conflicted with them. So, my current opinions and perspectives are a bit different from the ones I had back in 1990 and 1991.

Generally speaking, prophet-type spirits have a propensity to predict misfortunes and tragedies. This is what I came to

---

* Rear Heaven consists of realms inhabited by spirits that practice ascetic disciplines to attain supernatural and psychic powers. The inhabitants include magicians, wizards, and sorcerers.

realize after observing not one or two, but many spirits. It seems that people from Rear Heaven like to predict future calamities but often suffer severe persecution and oppression. For example, Oomoto, a Japanese religion originating from Shinto, prophesied the bombing of Tokyo during World War II, saying that there would be a hail of fire. Although this prophecy later came true, Oomoto was nevertheless persecuted by the government.

No one is happy to see tragic predictions come true. Even if the prediction of a tragedy doesn't come true, the prophet is harshly criticized for being wrong. And when it takes a long time for a prophecy to be fulfilled, people sometimes grow impatient and start persecuting the people who believe the prophecy. Regardless of whether a prophecy will come true or not, predicting negative events doesn't lead to positive outcomes.

These prophet-type spirits usually give negative predictions. Some of their prophecies come true, and others don't. The reason why some predictions don't come to pass is that there are people working to prevent negative prophecies from being fulfilled.

One problem with prophesying negative events is that people often misunderstand and think that the prophet himself wants the terrible thing to happen. This is why I decided that it would be better to refrain from making negative predictions. I took back any prophecies of doom I had previously made, and I haven't made any predictions of this sort since the end of the 1990s.

*"Throughout history, each religious group has been engaging in fierce competition, trying to become a majority force in the world."*

Spirits in heaven offer me all different sorts of opinions. But since Happy Science is held responsible for the opinions I take in, I feel that it's necessary to filter out the ones that I wouldn't be able to take responsibility for.

The spirits that guide Islam have ideas of their own and often clash with Christian spirits. These two spirit groups are engaging in a tug-of-war in heaven, just as Republicans and Democrats confront each other in the United States Congress. To be more precise, just as there are multiple political parties in the Japanese Diet, there are several powers in heaven. And throughout history, each religious group has been engaging in fierce competition, trying to become a majority force in the world.

In this context, we at Happy Science cannot take in all the different ideas equally from each group. The future of Happy Science may depend on which ideas and opinions we agree with, so since the end of the 1990s, I've been taking a slightly different approach.

> *"Anglo-Saxon civilization,*
> *merged with Christianity, is*
> *the most dominant civilization*
> *in the world today."*

Most prophet-type spirits have been born in the desert regions of the world, known today as countries such as Iran, Iraq, Kuwait, Saudi Arabia, Lebanon, Israel, and Egypt. Many spirits in this group laud the revival of Islam and the resurgence of Islamic power.

Islam was founded by Muhammad in the seventh century, well after the rise of Christianity. At one time, Islamic civilization enjoyed a period of dominance over Christian civilization. Islamic civilization flourished due to advances in mathematics and science during the Middle Ages, when Christian civilization entered a declining period known as the Dark Ages.

During this period, the Christian Church heavily criticized and nearly erased the works of Aristotle, saying that they posed a threat to the Christian faith. But his works were translated into Arabic and studied by Muslim philosophers, scientists, and scholars. In the twelfth and thirteen centuries, his works stored in

Spain were translated into Latin and revived interest in Aristotle in Christian culture.

So in some respects, Islamic civilization was superior to Christian civilization during the Middle Ages. But Christianity made a remarkable comeback and regained its power with the emergence of Protestantism in the modern era. Following the industrial revolution, Christian nations became more powerful, leading Christian civilization to become predominant on a global scale for the past two or three hundred years.

Today, Christian civilization, especially that led by the Anglo-Saxons, is definitely the most prominent civilization in the world. Anglo-Saxon civilization, merged with Christianity, is the most dominant civilization in the world today. In contrast, Islamic civilization has lost influence since the beginning of the modern era. Islam is now mainly spreading in Africa and other areas that were previously colonized by the West.

*"Japan's participation in the war triggered other Asian countries to declare independence."*

The Gulf War highlighted the big technological gap between the United States and Iraq. It was almost a one-sided battle in which American forces unilaterally launched attacks on the Iraqis. The Iraqi troops numbered approximately one million, while the U.S. forces had about two to three hundred thousand soldiers. By traditional standards of war, Iraq shouldn't have been defeated so easily, but contrary to their initial expectations, the Iraqis suffered a devastating defeat because they couldn't wage modern warfare. Iraq's war strategies were out of date, and America's modern weaponry put them at a serious disadvantage. Iraq suffered a similar fate in the Iraq War.

Half a century ago, Japan, another small country, fought against the United States. But the gap in technology and military strength between Japan and the United States at that time was much smaller than that between Iraq and the United States today. During World War II, Japan already had mobile tasks forces stationed mainly on aircraft carriers. Japan is actually the only country that has fought against America using domestically built aircraft carriers. Although Japan lost in the end and was reduced to ruins, Japan had the military strength to withstand four years of fierce battle against the United States.

Before World War II, Japan was extending its power vigorously, and this led to a battle for supremacy with the United States. Japan temporarily fell into a decline following its defeat but then started joining, to a great extent, the Western, Anglo-Saxon civilization. In fact, Japan had opened itself to Anglo-Saxon civilization before World War II, at the time of the Meiji Restoration in 1868. But back then, the Japanese only took in technology from the West, retaining in their hearts the proud conviction that Japan was superior to the Western world. The defeat in World War II made them realize that they needed to westernize their thinking and mindset to some degree. This is one of the ways that World War II was significant. It was at this point that Anglo-Saxon civilization secured a dominant position in the world.

But in another way, Japan gained a victory over the Anglo-Saxons. Japan's participation in the war triggered other Asian countries that had previously been colonized by Western countries such as Great Britain, France, and the Netherlands to declare independence. So it was not actually a total victory for Anglo-Saxon civilization; it also became a call for the Western nations to reflect on their past conduct.

*"War is a key factor in determining which civilization is dominant in a given time period."*

On a macro level, it seems to me that war is a key factor in determining which civilization is dominant in a given time period. With Islam spreading in Asia, the number of Muslims worldwide has reached more than a billion. So some people believe that Muslims now outnumber Christians. In fact, quite a few of Islam's high spirits intend to encroach on America. But the current clash between Christian civilization and Islamic civilization isn't about numbers of followers; it's about differences in these two religions' teachings.

World War II was actually a religious conflict between the Japanese Shinto-based civilization and the Anglo-Saxon Christian civilization. Both America and Japan fought with solid religious backbones. The Japanese Shinto gods did not budge an inch, but when the two spiritual forces fought against each other, the Shinto lost the war.

A similar conflict took place between America and Iraq. The Iraq War was a battle for religious superiority between two countries with different religious backgrounds. Former president George W. Bush unwittingly made a remark that upset some people by likening the operations in Iraq to the Crusades. It was a slip of the tongue, but it probably came from his heart; he wanted to bring an end to this conflict.

> # "The current American civilization is a combination of Judean and Christian civilizations."

The current American civilization is a combination of Judean and Christian civilizations. Jews control the financial circles and mass media, which are the axis of the United States. This explains why America is in battle with the anti-Semitic Arabs.

The desert regions of the Middle East were predominantly under Islamic influence. But the Jews came in, created a nation called Israel, and expelled other ethnic groups from the area. The Arabs were outraged by their conduct and have been seeking to banish the Jews from the land. For the Arabs, it was as if a stranger showed up one day and built a house on their property. Based on their logic and also from a religious perspective, it's probably only natural for them to get upset by what the Jews did. And in terms of demographics, too, the Arabs clearly predominate in that region.

However, Israel is a very powerful country because it has the support of the United States. Some believe that Israel has the world's second most powerful military forces, following America, because although it's a small country, it has money, technology, and nuclear weapons. So, it wouldn't be easy for the surrounding Arabian nations to destroy Israel. Even if the Arab nations were to declare war on Israel, they would most likely be defeated.

The difference in their national strength lies in the technological gap between these countries. Israel has acquired the money, knowledge, and advanced technology to make up for its small population. It's this big gap in technology that will most likely cause their defeat should the Arabs wage war against Israel. Furthermore, Israel has joined forces with the United States, which makes it even more likely that the Arabs would be defeated if they engaged in a military clash against Israel or America for the cause of Islam. Saddam Hussein was hailed by the Arabs as the first hero since Saladin, but he lost to U.S. forces because he tried to fight with only "horses and swords." Iran and Lebanon will probably face the same fate if they engage in war.

*"America will probably remain strong at least to the end of the twenty-first century."*

Islamic nations are technologically behind Western nations by fifty to one hundred years, or even longer in some respects. With the defeat in World War II, Japan realized that the country that lagged behind in technological advancement would not be able to win a war against a technologically advanced nation. A similar fate awaits the Islamic nations, and their defeat will bring about a reformation movement.

At a global level, it seems that the deities that guide the Western world are taking a little lead over the high spirits of Islam. If they engage in a fierce battle, neither side will achieve a complete victory or suffer a complete defeat, but the outcome will make it clear which civilization will be the dominant force. And as a result, I anticipate that a revolutionary movement will occur in the Islamic nations.

It's true that Great Britain and other Western countries need to make amends for the atrocious acts they committed during their colonial days. But they're currently facing a second wave of trials caused by the lack of technological advancement of the countries that became independent after World War II. This is the bigger picture of the world today.

In the past, I've touched on the possibility of the downfall of the United States, because I wanted to respect the opinions of the Japanese Shinto gods and the Arabic high spirits. But, at this point, objective observation of the current state of affairs reveals that the Anglo-Saxon gods still retain powerful leadership and exercise strong spiritual force in the world. So it's hard to imagine that they will become a minor power while the Arabic or Asian nations take the reins of the world during the twenty-first century.

It's unlikely that we'll see America's downfall any time soon. America will probably remain strong at least to the end of the twenty-first century.

> *"Japan can fulfill the role of helping other Asian countries and the desert regions reconstruct their civilization and flourish."*

It will probably take about a hundred years for Japan to completely recover from the damage inflicted by the defeat in World War II. Japan needs a little more time before it can exercise global leadership and share its values with the world. But Japan is going through a gradual and steady change and is coming close to becoming the world's second most powerful country. I believe that Japan, as a nation of a nonwhite race, can fulfill the role of helping other Asian countries and the desert regions reconstruct their civilization and flourish while working with the United

States. It would be best for Japan, as a leading Asian nation, to provide help and support to reform other Asian countries that have lagged behind in some areas, while at the same time cooperating with America.

While a part of the Muslim world enjoys prosperity, for the most part, it has fallen behind, bound by its out-of-date customs and laws. It would be to these nations' advantage if they can open themselves up to different perspectives and outside ideas and learn from them. India also needs to organize its ancient religious traditions and beliefs. If the magnetic force of the antique religions remains too strong, the country may continue to suffer from a series of misfortunes and tragedies.

Currently, Japan has a considerable economic impact on China. In the near future, Japan will increase its influence over this atheistic and socialistic power as it goes through a change. I envision Japan becoming a model nation for Asia.

*"It would be best for Japan to cooperate with the United States."*

As I've said, America will remain the central civilization throughout the twenty-first century. So I think it would be best for Japan to cooperate with the United States. The Japanese people who are against stronger ties between Japan and America simply do not see the trend of the times. They're repeating the same mistake as those who were embroiled in the struggle against the Japan-U.S. Security Treaty back in the 1960s and 1970s. Failing to cooperate with the United States would hinder Japan's prosperity. Japan should keep up with the flow of the global trend.

It will be great news if China becomes a capitalistic country based on market principles. The best-case scenario would be for China to become a capitalist nation, North Korea to become a free nation, and Japan, the Korean Peninsula, China, Australia, and all the surrounding nations in Southeast Asia to prosper under a shared set of values. I also hope that the Muslim world will be gradually revitalized by opening up to a variety of different perspectives and ideas. From an overall perspective, this is the direction that will bring about a positive impact on Earth's civilizations, and this is what we should aim for.

# CHAPTER THREE

# How *to* Overcome Stress

# I.

# *The* Art *of* Achieving Success *with a* Calm Mind

# 20. How to Overcome Fatigue, Frustration, and Gloominess

### QUESTION

I am a corporate employee and often get stressed out or feel down at work. How can I overcome these feelings?

# ANSWER

> *"With only a minute of deep breathing, you can calm your mind considerably."*

I f you're working in a busy office, you probably have to meet many people and answer a lot of phone calls in your day-to-day work life. You could work as happily as a clam if only you didn't have to answer the phone all day long. But against your wishes, the phone keeps ringing off the hook. To make the situation worse, when you pick up the phone, the person on the other end of the line complains about your products and services. When you receive one troublesome call after another, you get more and more irritated and may start to take out your frustration on the people around you.

If you're constantly busy, fatigue gradually accumulates and often negatively affects your state of mind. So it's important to take breaks and check in on your state of mind several times a day. If you find yourself making harsh remarks to others or find that your mind is becoming disturbed, I recommend that you leave your desk and go somewhere else, like the restroom, and take deep breaths. With only a minute of deep breathing, you can calm your mind considerably.

You can also look at yourself in the mirror and see if your face looks tired or grim. If it does, smile at your reflection in the mirror and encourage yourself to do your best for the rest of the day and get back to work. If an hour or two passes and you find yourself becoming stressed out again, step out for a bit to repeat the same process.

As you repeatedly check in with yourself and make the effort to change your mood this way, you start to be able to put yourself into a positive mood quickly, in just five to ten seconds. The moment you find yourself irritated, you'll automatically take deep breaths and smile, and that will instantly snap you out of your negative mood.

> *"Creating a positive and cheerful aura will make others believe that something good has happened to you."*

If you have to visit your client in bad weather to sell your products, you might feel gloomy and reluctant, especially if you know that the chances are you'll be turned down. Not wanting to face another rejection, you might walk around the office, hoping that no one is there. And instead of going into the office, you might just go into a nearby coffee shop. This may be the reason why coffee shops do well on rainy days.

If you find yourself in this kind of situation, imagine that you're an actor playing the role of a happy, successful salesperson. Go into the building and enter the office with a big smile. Your clients will come up to you and ask repeatedly if something good has happened to make you smile. When you have a smile on your face, people take keen notice and develop an interest in what you have to say, because they're more accustomed to hearing bad news and so are often desperately in need of good news.

Creating a positive and cheerful aura will make others believe that something good has happened to you. And if you hint at it saying, "I'll let you know later," and leave the office without telling them anything specific, they might come visit you to see if you're ready to share the good news with them.

> *"Making a change in your appearance can help you feel better on the inside."*

There are days when, on top of bad weather, you don't feel well, and it seems like there is nothing you can do to snap out of your gloomy mood. At times like these, try wearing bright-colored clothes to boost your mood. For example, you can put on a red tie and give yourself a little smile in the mirror before stepping out the door. The color red has the effect of making you feel excited, which helps revitalize your mood. In this way, when you can't change your inner self, try making a change on the outside. Making a change in your appearance can help you feel better on the inside as well.

Another way to improve your mood when you're feeling down is to find a happy smile on the face of someone else. This often works. You can also improve your mood by listening to someone else tell a good story. These are some methods you can use to overcome fatigue, frustration, and gloominess. As long as you keep trying, I'm sure you will find a way out of a negative mood.

# 21. How to Maintain Inner Peace When You're Busy

**QUESTION**

How can I maintain inner peace while I'm doing many things at once, like the thousand-armed Avalokitesvara (the goddess of mercy) who can handle a thousand tasks at the same time?

> *"The most capable members of the business elite probably have a hard time concentrating their minds."*

While it would be ideal if you could do a thousand things at the same time like the thousand-armed goddess of mercy, very few people in the world can do this. Things don't usually work out that way. Even if you're enthusiastic about your work and want to take on a lot of different projects, in reality, you face many limitations that prevent you from fulfilling that wish. So for most people, it's probably best to try to do the work of four hands or five at most instead of a thousand. You may be able to accomplish some extra work, as if you had additional feet and an extra mouth, but that's probably the most you can hope for.

Busy go-getters tend to be always on the move, keeping their mouths, hands, and feet very busy. They also keep their minds full and easily get stressed out. But these people are often the most capable members of the business elite. If people like this try to meditate at one of our Happy Science centers or temples, they'll probably have a hard time concentrating their minds. It's almost painful to watch how they struggle with quiet contemplation. Although these elite businesspeople see themselves as competent and excellent workers, when it comes to meditation, they seem completely incompetent.

> *"It's essential to create a time and space to maintain a calm state of mind."*

The human brain emits alpha waves and beta waves. Alpha waves are released when the mind is serene, like the placid surface of a lake. Beta waves, on the other hand, are emitted when the mind is busy and cluttered. Competent and busy businesspeople often release beta waves from their brains and, unfortunately, it is not easy to make the switch from beta waves to alpha waves. When these people come to meditate at a Happy Science center, they can't get away from the bustle of everyday work. They constantly look at their watches, unable to concentrate their minds. Other participants who can concentrate their minds may find their presence annoying.

People of this type have a hard time breaking free of the busyness because it has become a mental habit. They are always in a hurry, rushing to get to work before everyone else. Every morning, they push through crowds of people to board jam-packed commuter trains. Although they don't necessarily like their jobs, they feel pressed to get to work as early as they can. A habit like this, when it's built over a long period of time, gets ingrained in the mind and is very difficult to break. I would hope, though, that these people would leave this habit at the door when they attend our meditation seminars. The types of people that these go-getters look down on as incapable at work can become much more capable than them when it comes to concentrating their minds. It would actually serve these busy people well to receive a stern reprimand and spiritual shakeup to clear their minds. These people have paid a price for their success in business; they've lost sight of something important somewhere along the way.

People don't change easily, and they probably can't change the type of work they do either. But it's essential to create a time and space to maintain a calm state of mind. By making the effort to go to a quiet place or take the time to concentrate their minds, they'll learn to shift their mental gears.

The same goes for our missionary activities. Some members of Happy Science are afraid that they might lose their peace of mind if they're negatively influenced by the people they talk to. It's possible for talking to others to disturb your peace of mind, especially if the people you're trying to share the Truths with are under the influence of negative spirits. So missionary work can wear you out. But this is the very time for you to improve your state of mind through such spiritual practices as reading the books of Truths, listening to the audio recordings of my lectures, or reflecting on your mind. As you accumulate experiences and get used to doing missionary work, you'll feel your mind becoming more stable and tranquil as if it's transforming itself from a small puddle to a large lake. And you'll be less susceptible to negative influences from others.

> *"Consider the fatigue and distress you experience as the tax you pay for living in this world."*

While we live in this world, we sometimes have to go through times of being busy with work, which can disturb our peace of mind. But we should think of this as a type of tax we need to pay for our life in this world. You may wish to spend all your time meditating, but that's probably not possible. The busyness of everyday life serves as the tax you pay for living in this world.

Busy people will need to learn how to quiet down their state of mind. The busier they are, the more important it is to take quiet time to look within. You may think that your mind would be at ease if you had enough money to live on without having to work. But sooner or later, you'd become restless and start worrying that you'd been abandoned by society, and that would make you want to start working again.

Human beings wish for what they can't have. When we lead a busy life, we wish to take it easy and enjoy peace and quiet in solitude. But when our wish is granted, we can't bear having no social interaction. So I believe we should do some type of work, although when we do, our peace of mind will inevitably be disturbed. Just as we have to pay taxes, we need to bear this burden as part of living in this world.

Businesses often have to pay about half the profits they make as taxes, and their income after tax is their on-target earnings. Similarly, when you work, consider your work as your contribution to the world and the fatigue and distress you experience as the tax you pay for living in this world. Even if you have to pay half your earnings as taxes, the remaining half will be pure profit, which you'll be able to keep. The amount of profit you can make will depend on the extent of your spiritual practice. So the more busy and difficult your life is, the more essential it becomes to train your mind through self-reflection, prayer, and other spiritual practices.

# 22. How to Tell When We're Reaching Too Far

**QUESTION**

I've learned at Happy Science that
our strong desires will come true,
but that when they grow overly strong,
they could destroy us, so we should live
within the limits of our ability.
How can I tell if I've let my desires
grow too strong?

# ANSWER

*"When you reach too far, many setbacks and adversities start happening to you."*

I f you want to know where to draw the line between reasonable desires and excessive desires, you first need to know yourself. It all comes down to the battle of knowing yourself.

When you reach too far, many setbacks and adversities start happening to you. For example, when you overwork yourself, you may fall sick. Even though you're not wishing to get sick, for some reason you come down with a cold, develop a fever, and are forced to stay in bed. In some cases, you feel perfectly healthy, but someone in your family may fall sick. If you come under a lot of stress at work, your children may start causing trouble. Children who are affected by their parents' stress may become delinquent and get into trouble with teachers and classmates at school.

Families often bear a heavy burden, especially in the cases of successful business executives and people of high position in society. Even if people who are under a lot of pressure aren't aware of it themselves, those around them, including their spouses, children, and parents, could well be affected by their stress. These people need to pay attention to the conditions of their family members at all times. But people who are the type to go headlong into their goal without considering the circumstances around them often have no idea what's going on with their family members.

If you know someone who falls into this category, try this simple exercise. Wait until about 3:00 in the afternoon and ask him if his wife put on makeup this morning, and if she did, ask him if he remembers the color of her lipstick. Then ask him if he remembers what she was wearing today and whether it was different from what she wore yesterday. Chances are that he won't be able to answer these questions, because he probably can't remember any of it. There is simply no way that this type of person knows the issues his family members are struggling with. In fact, he probably refuses to listen to his family's problems.

This type of person comes home late at night and rarely has conversations with his family. The only things he says are "What's for dinner?" "I'm taking a shower," and "I'm going to bed." The only time his wife can talk to him may be when he's in the bathroom, and he may get upset at being bombarded with questions. He spends most weekends on the golf course and is almost never home. The only thing he does for his family is pay the bills. He has no interest in how his wife and children are doing, so naturally, he fails to notice any changes or problems at home.

What usually happens to people like him, as the world goes, is at some point they begin to face setbacks. They stop getting promoted and instead get demoted to an unimportant position or shunted off to a remote area, which finally gives them time to reflect on themselves. In rare cases, they go all the way to the top of the corporate ladder straightaway, only to find themselves with a dysfunctional family. Even if they avoid a family breakup, something unfavorable will happen to someone or something else close to them. A wise person would notice these things before they reached a crisis point.

> *"Becoming sick is often a sign that our bodies are in need of repairs."*

The first thing you can do to see whether you have excessive desires is check your physical condition. If you have a lot of health problems, it may well be a sign that your desires for self-realization at work and in other areas may have grown too strong.

Your physical condition is partly governed by your subconscious, which is usually hidden under your conscious mind. When you push yourself too far, your body starts showing signs of impairment. The first sign is probably a cold. Haruchika Noguchi, a Japanese therapist and founder of *Seitai* (osteopathy and chiropractic therapies), taught about the benefits of colds. According to Noguchi, a cold can prevent a fundamental breakdown of our bodies.

On average, we catch a cold a couple of times a year and feel unwell for about three days to a week. This is our bodies telling us to take a break. It's a primal signal from the deeper part of our existence, saying, "Your body will break down unless you take a rest now!" So part of the reason we catch a cold is that our bodies need a rest and a chance to put themselves back in order. It's like getting our cars repaired. Becoming sick is often a sign that our bodies are in need of repairs. So if you notice a change in your physical condition, that's a good opportunity for you to reflect on where you've gone wrong.

> *"An increased number of complaints*
> *may be a sign that*
> *you're going to extremes."*

Another essential point to consider is whether you're getting an increased number of complaints about your work. If you're in sales, for example, setting your target too high and pushing yourself to achieve it may draw a stream of complaints. An increased number of complaints may be a sign that you're going to extremes and making wrong decisions that cause others trouble.

The proper handling of complaints is crucial to business management. We need to handle complaints with care, because companies that disregard the voices of their customers won't last. Your customers will complain if you push your product at them by presenting it as if it's an excellent product when it isn't. As you're forced to deal with dissatisfied customers, your sales will decline. This happens when you deviated from the Middle Way in your work and go too far. Declining health and increasing complaints are both signs that you don't want to miss.

> *"You need to notice the signs of potential problems before they actually occur."*

Additionally, when you push yourself too much at work, you'll start having problems at home such as your family members falling ill. If you fail to notice these signs early on, you may be faced with divorce, and this may in turn negatively affect your performance at work to an even greater extent.

World-renowned business magnate Jack Welch, who rebuilt General Electric, is often seen as a savior or reviver of the global enterprise. But he had to end his marriage with his former wife when he was fifty-two years old because he was married to his job. He neglected his family and was hardly ever home. Even on weekends, he would spend most of his time playing golf with business associates.

Welch fired an incredible number of employees, one after another. I can imagine him coming home at night after firing thousands of employees; he probably had a fierce aura like that of a soldier with disheveled hair dragging a bloody sword off the battlefield. It must have been an unbearable burden for his former wife to deal with such stress. Home is a place where we can release stress, but the level of stress Welch brought home was not something that an average person could handle. That's why his wife left him.

After the divorce, Welch's former wife went back to school and became a lawyer. She got remarried, to someone she met at college, and they began practicing law together. Welch also got married again. This time, he had his wife take golf lessons so they could play together, but she ended up leaving him too. As in Welch's example, business success and a happy home often don't go hand in hand, and this imbalance is often a sign that we are stretching ourselves a little too far.

Even if you succeed at work, you may face serious issues at home. You need to notice the signs of potential problems before they actually occur. You may fail to recognize them if you're too focused on yourself, so it's important to pay close attention to the feelings of people around you.

> *"The Principles of Progress and Self-Reflection balance each other out, leading us into the right path."*

To summarize, the signs of overwork include declining health, an increased number of complaints about your work, and family problems. If you notice these things happening to you, you need to hold yourself back. This is an essential practice if you want to fulfill your responsibilities at work.

For example, a popular author writing for a dozen magazines every month is probably overdoing it. If she ends up getting sick and is hospitalized, she won't be able to live up to her responsibilities as a writer. But when she goes too far, she should see signs of potential danger, such as her spouse complaining that she never has time for her family. If she can take notice of these signs and listen to her spouse, she should be able to reflect on herself and change the way she works.

The principle of progress that I teach at Happy Science is not about going headlong to achieve as much as you can. I also teach the principle of self-reflection, which is about the importance of reflecting on ourselves and correcting our path when we're not doing well. These two principles of progress and self-reflection balance each other out, leading us into the right path.

There's a limit as to how far we can go. If your desires grow too strong, you need to curb them. This is a timeless topic that each person has to deal with. I hope you can use the ideas I've discussed here as guidelines to check on yourself.

# II.

# *The* Art *of* Making Good Decisions *at* Work

# 23. Overcoming Slumps at Work

**QUESTION**

I work in a managerial position, and I sometimes suddenly find myself in a slump when I've been through an intense period of work. What causes these slumps, and what can I do to prevent them?

ANSWER

## "You should start planning in advance to take some days off."

The most common everyday cause of a slump at work is overworking yourself. When you feel a slump coming on, take time to evaluate your current physical, mental, and intellectual condition. Then look through and reconsider your schedule and plans for the next one to four weeks. If your workload is more than you can reasonably handle in your present condition, your only true option is to take time off. When what's on your plate right now looks overwhelming in light of the condition you're in, you should start planning in advance to take some days off.

We definitely face some times in our lives when we can't avoid working around the clock. But to perform well in your work consistently over the course of many years, it's vitally important to take enough time off. If you fall behind, you can make up for it another day.

Imagine yourself as an airplane. You'll work far more efficiently if you take the time to land your aircraft, refuel, check its condition, and then take flight again than you will by flying on low fuel, wobbling just barely above the ground. Practice giving yourself enough time to take a break—this is an important pearl of wisdom to remember.

> *"Perfectionists are convinced that they're the only ones that can handle their work."*

People who frequently find themselves in a slump tend to be perfectionists who eagerly handle everything on their own. The stronger this tendency is in them, the more prone they are to facing slumps. If you're prone to perfectionism, you should check whether you're truly the only one who can best handle your job and whether you might be robbing others of their work.

Often, perfectionists are convinced that they're the only ones that can handle their work and overexert themselves, when in truth, they either lack the skills to delegate their work to others, are hogging the work, or need to approach their work with more wisdom. Even if they think they're working extremely hard, it's not uncommon to find that they're actually depriving others of work.

Some people in managerial positions, for example, have a working style that makes their physical presence absolutely necessary for things to run smoothly. When a manager like this is away on vacation, his subordinates don't know what to do and have no choice but to ask his callers to wait until his return. A manager who runs his section in this way may actually be robbing his subordinates of work.

It's definitely important to put your best into the work you do, but that's not all there is to your job. Your job also requires that you take measures to prepare your section or department to operate relatively smoothly even when you're gone. Your subordinates need a system to fall back on when you can't be present, and creating such a system will benefit not only yourself, but also your subordinates and associates, as well as your company as a whole.

If you don't already have a system like this in place, you need to create one, or you're bound to face panic in the future. You need to establish a plan that will make it possible for your responsibilities to be met even without you. You want to be prepared with a secondary backup plan, as well, should the initial one fail. It's crucial to have a system prepared in advance, so that if you ever suddenly fall ill, your subordinates and colleagues won't have to suddenly get together to discuss what to do.

> ## *"The superiors' role is to entrust their subordinates with work."*

It's important to acknowledge the different purposes that different people have in this world. Not only are there car mechanics who repair limousines; there are also limousine drivers, and business executives who ride them, and all these various roles are meant to be fulfilled by different people. What's truly crucial, then, is not to continue working to your maximum by yourself, but to assign work to others and nurture them through administering training.

The superiors' role is to entrust their subordinates with work, and a superior who refuses to do so is not truly fostering their subordinates' growth. Assigning work to others is not a form of punishment, but a way of teaching them and nurturing their abilities.

The superiors' role, then, is also about guiding their subordinates to grow. Superiors should think of ways to help their subordinates develop their capabilities, such as their decision-making abilities. One way to do this is to ask them for their own views or explain to them something that you've read in a book, when your subordinates ask you questions, instead of simply answering them. This will get them to think about their question. And, later on, you can also recommend a book for them to read, so that they can continue to contemplate their question. You don't need to solve all the problems that are brought to your desk. Sometimes, giving your subordinates important hints is more than enough.

Some superiors become deeply involved whenever they're approached for advice, and a month may pass before they realize how much time they've spent solving the subordinate's problem. This may not always be an act of true love, if it slows your subordinate's ability to bounce back, slows the pace of your own work, and diminishes the time and energy you're able to give others.

Rather than joining in on the problem, give your subordinate words of guidance to help her get back on her feet. Doing so will not only lighten the load of your own work, but will also foster your subordinate's growth. It may also help you and your subordinate avert a slump.

The same principle holds true when you find yourself in a slump. If you're mostly just wishing for others to help you, you'll probably find it difficult to find your way out of it. But if you make up your mind to face it yourself, you'll find the solution eventually. And the accomplishment of finding your way out of your slump will further empower you, and that's why finding your own way out is so important.

> *"There is a type of a slump that's caused by spiritual disturbances."*

Aside from a typical type of slump, there is also a slightly different type of a slump that's caused by spiritual disturbances. A spiritual disturbance is a condition caused by some form of negative spiritual influence. Many people suffer from negative spiritual influences, so it's not uncommon to find yourself picking some up in your interactions with others.

When you're in this state, you may suffer from a strong sense of unhappiness and feelings of depression. Your outlook on the world and the future may turn bleak, you may feel as if things are bound to get worse, and you may not be able to help having very pessimistic thoughts. Physically, you may feel very listless, easily irritated, and grumpy. You may make poor judgments, lose decisiveness, and you may put off making decisions. You may also begin to see others negatively. For instance, you might distrust others' ability to handle the jobs you've delegated to them. You may distrust people around you and want to do everything all by yourself. But no matter how hard you work, you don't make much progress. You then sink deeper into your sense of distrust and even start to lose faith in God, which sinks you deeper into your slump.

If you experience these symptoms, you should suspect that a spiritual disturbance is the likely cause. These cases are often not just caused by a weakened physical condition from overexertion at work. We humans sometimes need to recognize that we are neither Superman nor Wonder Woman, but just normal humans who inevitably experience slumps from time to time. So when we notice the signs of an impending slump, we need to be mindful of our condition and begin taking measures to help ourselves deal with it well.

# 24. Making the Right Decision

**QUESTION**

Sometimes at work, I feel lost in a sea of choices. How do I make the best possible decisions in that situation?

## ANSWER

> ### *"Look at each opinion and figure out which ones are truly better than the others."*

It can be very difficult to tell which of the many options in front of you is the best one when the level of your awareness is still not high. All the opinions you've listened to probably sound as though they're sound and would be the right decisions. Cultivating a higher level of awareness, however, will help you clearly distinguish the differences between them.

First, gaining a higher level of awareness will help you understand why different opinions have come up. Next, you'll develop a better understanding of each of the opinions themselves. And not only will you understand them better; you'll also be able to distinguish the ones with a higher perspective or more right way of thinking from the others.

We can find a kernel of Truth within every opinion that exists in this world. If we look at the world of politics, for instance, we find a numerous array of political parties competing with one another, but the principle that each party stands for holds a grain of Truth. But, while all of them may appear equally valuable to our human understanding, it's very clear from God's perspective which ones are more outstanding than the others. So before you make a decision about which opinion to choose, I recommend looking at each opinion in front of you and figuring out which ones are truly better than the others.

*"Ask yourself what God would want you to do in this situation."*

If you turn to other people for help, all of their opinions will probably sound right to you. So if you want to know which one of them offers the better way of thinking, you can't allow other people's opinions to sway your thinking. You need to calm the state of your mind and choose the Middle Way, the middle path of avoiding extremes, and then consider each of the options in light of the Truths.

Put another way, it's important to ask yourself what God would want you to do in this situation. Which of the choices in front of you would God prefer? He wouldn't pick multiple answers; he always makes one decision. There will always be one choice that sits closest to God's way of thinking. Finding your way to this choice is part of your spiritual training in this world.

For example, we're often told that we are given freedom as humans. If we were to take this idea at face value, we would behave in any way that pleased us, regardless of where we were. And yet, we still choose to behave properly and with good manners if we, for example, go to attend a seminar, even though we're aware that that restricts our freedom. Why do we choose to do this? Because we understand that there are other people aside from ourselves in the audience who also came to listen to the seminar. This is why we choose not to give in to sudden urges to sing out loud while the speaker is talking. There's nothing wrong with the act of singing in and of itself, but we know that it's the wrong way to behave in the middle of a seminar.

It's easy to understand the point that I'm trying to make in an example like this one, but since we're all human, it's not always as easy to choose the best option in real life. This can indeed be difficult to do, but what's really important is that, each time, we continue to look for the one that lies closer to God's will.

> *"People who have made more decisions
> that are close to God's heart will
> attain a higher spiritual level."*

To find the choices that lie closer to God's will, we need to learn as much as we can from the books of Truths and base our decisions on them. We need to look at the Truths in these books as our basis for making the best possible decisions. It's the sum of the choices you make in this life that proves what kind of person you've been and determines which spiritual level you're destined for in the afterlife. People who have made more decisions that are close to God's heart will attain a higher spiritual level, and those with less of these decisions will reach a lower spiritual level.

Whatever the outcome may be for you, you're the only one who can take responsibility for your choices, and in the end, you need to rely upon yourself to make the best decisions you possibly can. Each of these decisions individually may look insignificant to you. But as you make each decision with a heart as close to God's as possible, and as these decisions accumulate, I am certain that you'll eventually get to a high spiritual state. How much time it takes to do so depends on each individual. It may take several years for some, and several cycles of rebirth for others, but even if it takes thousands or tens of thousands of years, the most important thing you must do is never give up.

# 25. Solving Issues During Tough Times in Business

## QUESTION

I have a hard time sleeping, because our business is going through a downturn. Is there anything I can do to sleep better?

## ANSWER

> *"We often go through periods of poor sleep when the storms of life assail us."*

We often go through periods of poor sleep when the storms of life assail us. And when this sleeplessness continues for a long time, some type of spiritual influence is usually at work. But we can take comfort in one thing: no one has ever died of sleep deprivation before.

When we realize that we have an ongoing sleep issue, we might start to panic, but not only has no one ever died of insomnia; we're also physically incapable of staying awake for more than several days at a time, so we can rest assured that we'll fall asleep eventually. So if you're worried about periods of sleeplessness, remember: sleep deprivation is not a life-threatening issue.

Often, when we're suffering from sleeplessness, it's because we're dealing with an overwhelming tangle of worries. Some people can comfortably deal with two problems, but throwing a third one into the mix would make things unbearable. Others can manage three problems at once, but a fourth could make things impossible to handle. At any given moment, each of us has a capacity for dealing with a certain number of problems.

> *"Analyze the problem objectively and gather essential information and ideas."*

The emotions of a business executive in a downturned company are in a state of confusion. The executive oscillates between working frantically on one project or another and wanting to give up. But to stop these oscillations, you need to analyze the problem objectively and gather essential information and ideas. When seen from an objective standpoint, you are confused because you can't clearly see a process that will get you from the current situation to the solution. You're grappling in agony because you're trying to make a decision without adequate information. When you don't have the necessary information, you're apt to think of things from a subjective perspective, but you won't be able to find the right conclusion in this way.

## *"Get to the root of the problem."*

The type of information you'll need to find is the kind that will lead you to a clear decision. You need to dig up the element that's at the heart of your decision. For example, whenever you're trying to decide whether to continue your current business, develop a new one, or fold an unprofitable department, there is always some key element or core factor that determines which option is best. This is the information that you need to find.

When you're having difficulty making a decision, you're often letting the tree's mangle of branches and leaves conceal the trunk from your view. You need to clear these things away to get a clear view of the trunk. The same idea applies when other people approach you with their problems. The advice you give them should help them weed out the leaves and branches so they can see the trunk; you want to help them get to the crux of their issue. Offering them this kind of advice will stop their worrying, and the rest will be a matter of making a choice.

Here's an example of what you might say:

"The key to solving your issue is *this*, which requires a yes or no decision. In your current circumstances, I recommend *this* decision, but you alone can make the final decision. Whatever you decide, honor your decision as faithfully as you can and don't let trifling matters distract and confuse you again. Do your utmost best to honor your decision unless you gain important, new information. And even if you find yourself facing very tough times in the process, remember that life gives you many opportunities for a fresh, new start."

Meanwhile, sleeping aids may help you for a while, but they aren't a long-term solution. What's most important is to get to the root of the problem and outline a clear line of thinking that will lead to a solution. Any decision we make always hinges on one crucial, determining factor. There is always just one most important element at the heart of a decision.

It's the person who can use this one crucial factor as a basis for decisions who is truly fit to be a leader and qualified to be an executive. I can't emphasize enough how important it is for leaders and executives to be able to identify the heart of any issue. It's difficult to fulfill a leadership role if you're constantly debating about the leaves and branches instead of the trunk. It's also natural for executives to be considerate of their employees' and other people's feelings. But as an executive, once you've found the heart of the problem and made a decision, you need to be able to tell your employees about your decision and ask them to follow you. You'll also need to prepare yourself to ask them to leave your company if they can't follow you.

*"Be prepared to face the worst-case scenario."*

You also need to be prepared to face the worst-case scenario, which I'm sure you'll be able to foresee. When worse comes to worst, you might lose your home and property, but you'll still be alive. Your home and property are assets that you've built over the course of ten to twenty years of hard work, so you can build these assets again with hard work. And not everyone will keep blaming you; you'll also find people who want to support you. Even in the worst-case scenario, you can always start over. As long as you have the will, you'll find a way. When you can find it in you to resolve on this, you'll stop worrying, and the only thing that will remain for you to do is take action.

## *"Live each day as if it were your last."*

When you're at your wit's end and feel completely lost, you can also break your time up into shorter periods and think about them like this:

"*This* is what I can do today, and *this* is what I'll work on tomorrow. In a week, I can start on *this*, and in a month, I can get to work on *that*. Am I worrying now about things that might happen in the future? Am I worrying about something that's not going to happen until a month from now? Or something I'll be working on six months or a year down the line? Or even something I won't have to face until I'm on my deathbed?"

This is when it becomes crucial to live each day as if it were your last, because everything always comes back to what you need to work on today. You can't work on something today that can only be done tomorrow. The only thing you can do right now is what you're capable of tackling today. This is the starting point that you need to come back to. Do what you can do today, but don't obsess about the future. Separate the problems you need to work on today from those you can best work on at some point in the future, and focus your mind on the things that you can get to work on today.

# III.

# *The* Art *of* Building *a* Deeper Sense *of* Self-Confidence

# 26. Overcoming Feelings of Inferiority

## QUESTION

I often waver between feeling inferior and superior to others. What should I do to overcome my inferiority complex?

# ANSWER

## *"Fighting this problem shouldn't be worth an entire lifetime of effort."*

I've taught before about the importance of examining our minds in depth to stop negative feelings, such as a sense of inferiority, from arising in our mind. But while this practice applies rather shallowly to a wide range of people, it's still a relatively basic stage of my teachings. As you progress in your study of the Truths, you'll eventually advance to the next stage, at which point it's time to learn and contemplate a wider variety of things.

The way I explain the Truths sometimes differs depending on who they're intended for. The teachings of the Truths come at various levels, from beginner to advanced, and the thinking behind each level is different because the people they're meant for are different.

Having said that, one problem with focusing on overcoming our sense of inferiority is that it makes us think only about ourselves. Those who suffer from feelings of inferiority tend to focus their thoughts only on themselves and rarely on others. What we need to do, then, is forget ourselves from time to time, broaden our view to the wider world, and find the desire within ourselves to help change the world.

Look at the vast world you live in that's giving you your life, and ask yourself how large your struggle with feelings of inferiority and superiority truly is. Asking yourself this question should help you realize how much of your precious time it really deserves. Spending time fighting this problem is not completely meaningless, but it shouldn't be worth an entire lifetime of effort. When the time comes to look back on your life, you may realize how unproductively you've lived if you've spent your whole life wavering between feelings of inferiority and superiority over others.

This struggle with an inferiority complex can be a necessary experience for our growth, but if we spend too much time on it, we'll miss out on a lot of important things. It's important to pull yourself out of those feelings as quickly as possible. Your life is precious, and it's vital that you think more about how to be more productive, proactive, and constructive in your life.

> *"Changing the way you think is one way of freeing yourself from your inferiority complex."*

No one is completely immune to the struggles of an inferiority complex. And much of the time, feelings of superiority just represent the other side of feelings of inferiority. If we kept searching, we'd find no end to the seeds of an inferiority complex. We don't realize this when we're only thinking about ourselves, but we can clearly see it when we look at others: everyone is struggling with their own various issues, and watching them absorbed like this makes you wish they'd forget about it, once and for all. When you see that you've been doing the same thing, you'll realize that you also need to let go of your inferiority complex.

Imagine a huge group of people as octopuses. They're all living inside individual pots that fishers have set out for them as traps and fighting their own feelings of inferiority. The longer they stay there, the more likely it is that the fishers will come hoist them up and catch them. All they need to do to escape is simply leave the trap, but instead they cling desperately to their pots, believing that there's danger outside, completely unaware of the greater danger they're putting themselves in by staying in their pots.

To escape, all the octopus has to do is let go of its grip of the walls, but its tentacles' suckers just keep on clinging. In the same way, some people cling to their struggle against feelings of inferiority and would do better to release their grip and go outside.

Like the octopus, they believe that the pot is a safe place to hide, where they'll be protected. They don't want to get hurt, they feel bad for themselves, and they believe they'll be safe as long as they stay inside their pots. What the pots represent in this analogy is your inner world that you've been submerged in so deeply.

Like the octopus stuck in its pot, you'll eventually be hoisted out of the depths of the water. The more you remain submerged in your inner world, the more you're putting yourself in danger's way. So what you truly need to do is make up your mind to leave your pot. My book, *Invincible Thinking** offers a teaching on revolutionizing your perspective, and using that teaching to change the way you think is one way to free yourself from your inferiority complex.

Instead of swaying to and fro between feelings of inferiority and superiority, you want to find a completely different path to lead you outside. By changing how you think, you'll be able to find a unique side of yourself, something you wouldn't have

---

* Ryuho Okawa, *Invincible Thinking* (New York: IRH Press, 2017).

seen if you stayed absorbed in comparisons between yourself and others—a facet of you that is wonderful and unique to you. It's so important that you love this aspect of yourself.

> *"When you find the solutions to your problems, you can be by other people's side as they struggle through theirs."*

Everyone experiences feelings of inferiority, so please don't feel that it's necessary to obsess over them. If you keep hiding inside your inferiority complex, like the octopus that never leaves its pot, you may end up spending your entire life slaving over this problem. Instead, strive to think like this:

"Have others before me suffered through similar problems? If I can find out what they've done to overcome their feelings of inferiority, maybe I can pick up some hints that will help me overcome my inferiority complex. And then maybe the people around me are facing a similar problem, and I'll be able to give them good advice to help them through it."

It's very important to start thinking this way. When you find the solutions to your problems, you're no longer absorbed in struggling through them. Instead, you can be by other people's side as they struggle through theirs. And that's when you know that you've finally left your own pot.

So don't keep your struggle with an inferiority complex to yourself; instead elevate it into something much more universal and objective, so that other people can use it as a basis for their own thinking. There are many ways you can heal your inferiority complex and many opportunities to share how you went about overcoming it.

If doing so gives rise to feelings of superiority over others, that's perfectly fine. This sense of superiority isn't wrong, because sharing your experiences with others will help make the world a better place. This is a righteous feeling of superiority. To sum up, everyone struggles with a sense of inferiority to some degree or other, but you won't be able to take the next step forward in your life until you're able to move on from it.

# 27. Finding an Unwavering Self-Confidence

**QUESTION**

I sometimes wonder whether my self-confidence has grown so much that I've become arrogant. How can I tell the difference between self-confidence and arrogance?

# ANSWER

> *"The difference between true self-confidence and arrogance manifests through your interactions with other people."*

T he basic attitude that's part of both a sense of self-confidence and arrogance is the sense that you excel at something, that you have an outstanding quality. There is nothing inherently wrong with having this sense of self-confidence. It is what motivates you to improve, and without it, you wouldn't be able to continue to grow as a person.

Of the two major guiding principles that govern the universe—progress and harmony—knowing that you have something outstanding definitely accords with the principle of progress. The sense that we are outstanding is, indeed, the original power from which we humans find the strength to grow that leads to the progress and prosperity of the world and the universe. Therefore, it is good to believe in your outstanding quality. You don't need to deny this sense of confidence.

But problems may arise, depending on the way you express this belief in your behavior and the shape of your actions. As we often say, evil does not exist in and of itself, but arises from a combination of different factors, including people, timing, and place. For example, it would be wrong for someone to go up on stage and start rehearsing a play in the middle of someone else's lecture. Nothing about rehearsing a play is inherently wrong, but we know that this isn't the appropriate timing and place for a rehearsal. In this way, our behavior itself isn't essentially wrong, but how our behavior combines with situational factors can make it inappropriate. The problem we find with confidence versus arrogance is extremely similar to this point I'm making.

If there were no one else around you, you could shout, "I am so incredible!" however often you wanted, but you'd have no way of knowing whether you were being confident or arrogant. The difference between true self-confidence and arrogance manifests through your interactions with other people. When your self-confidence is well-deserved, the people around you will think of you and say, "It's hard to describe it, but she is quite outstanding." But if others find your confidence unmerited and you're unaware of that, then it will appear as arrogance in their eyes.

> *"True self-confidence never wavers, regardless of the praise that other people receive."*

Here, I would like to talk about the factors that will help us distinguish between self-confidence and arrogance. People who've become arrogant are delighted to receive compliments but become disgruntled when they see others receiving them. This is especially true when the compliments pertain to a subject or area that interests the person. This is the clearest way to tell the difference between self-confidence and arrogance.

For example, if you feel confident about your public speaking skills but become unhappy when someone else receives recognition for public speaking, it could be a sign of false self-confidence. True self-confidence comes from a fair self-evaluation. It comes from a deep respect for yourself as a unique child of God—in other words, an awareness of your own unconditional value.

This is the reason why true self-confidence never wavers, regardless of the praise that other people receive. The kind of self-confidence that falters when other people are recognized for their abilities is not an authentic one. If this is the type of self-confidence you possess now, and you've been completely convinced that it's true self-confidence, then it's highly likely that it's actually a form of arrogance. So when you're trying to distinguish self-confidence from arrogance, one thing to look for is whether your confidence wavers when other people receive recognition.

> *"True confidence leads to giving love,*
> *and arrogance only leads to*
> *taking love from others."*

Another way of differentiating self-confidence from arrogance is to look at whether others find it unpleasant to be around you. If they do, it will serve you best to consider this a very obvious sign. In university classes, during student debates, sometimes one student takes up all the time and puts on a one-man show. All his classmates are put off by his behavior, but he doesn't seem to notice that they feel that way about him. Eventually, though, he's able to catch on when he notices his classmates constantly avoiding him, and he finally realizes that he must've been behaving too pridefully.

Avoidance is a type of spiritual response we receive from others that shows how our behavior has hurt other people's feelings. In other words, this happens to us when we've become overly aggressive toward others and treated them poorly, making them feel as though they're sitting on a bed of needles whenever they're around us.

This kind of response from others also indicates false confidence in yourself, because a truly confident person would want to support his peers. He would want to reach out to those who are not yet as outstanding as he is to offer them a chance to improve and grow into outstanding people themselves. Truly confident people are capable of helping others grow in a variety of ways.

If you're somehow hurting the feelings of those around you, it may be a sign that your confidence isn't authentic. This is a very clear way to tell whether or not your confidence is real. If you feel alienated and avoided by your peers at work, you may need to take it as a sign that you've been behaving arrogantly.

What I mean is that you might be craving others' love and respect, and your peers might be sensing your bottomless desire for love, as if you're waiting to sap them dry of their kindness. Some people have an aura of thirsting for recognition and praise, as if to say that they won't take no for an answer. It's difficult to deny these people, so those around them give them compliments. But when they do, it feels as if something has been taken away from them.

In the end, true confidence leads to giving love, and arrogance only leads to taking love from others. In the same way that rivers flow from higher to lower elevations, men and women who truly outshine others are capable of giving of themselves to others. And they're able to do so because of the true confidence they have in themselves. True confidence will lead you in the direction of giving of yourself to others, while false self-confidence will lead you in the opposite direction of seeking and concentrating on self-love. You'll need to look at which of these directions your mind is leaning toward.

*"Work toward achievements that bring you true fulfillment."*

The issue of self-confidence and arrogance is a problem that stalks everyone, no matter what grade of spirituality you have achieved. Even those who have a high level of enlightenment, a high degree of spiritual awareness, or a very large mission to fulfill in life will face this problem at some point in their lives. In fact, those with a higher soul level have a greater chance of coming up against this problem, since they're intrinsically aware that they excel at something. In an environment that limits them from realizing this side of themselves, however, they suffer. So they look to other people's praise for fleeting relief from this suffering.

We all go through such a stage at some point in life. If you find yourself in the middle of this period now, what you need to do is stop looking at recognition as a sign of accomplishment and instead work toward achievements that bring you true fulfillment. I feel that this is the most important thing you need to do to weather this difficulty. In addition, if you find others who are sharing the same experience, embrace them with kindness. Forgive them, with the acknowledgment that everyone goes through similar periods of difficulty, and with the understanding that even though they may be struggling right now, their souls will eventually overcome this challenge and they'll grow into the outstanding people they're meant to be.

If you imagine yourself as a *konpeito* candy (a lumpy sugar candy), then instead of working to remove these lumps, persevere to fill in the gaps between them so you can enlarge your caliber as a person. This task may take a lot of time to complete, but mindfully striving toward this goal will definitely help you get there. Don't look at your lumps as unwanted aspects of yourself in need of removal, because trying to remove them would only shrink your capacity as a person. Instead, make them disappear simply by enlarging the capacity of who you are. Enlarging your capacity will allow you to benefit far greater numbers of people than you could if you focused on trying to get rid of parts of yourself. I truly hope that you'll think of your arrogance in this light when you're faced with this period in life.

# 28. Living Lightheartedly and Selflessly

**QUESTION**

You have talked about the importance of living lightheartedly. What kinds of mindsets can we cultivate to help us live this way?"

# ANSWER

> *"We should strive to accept our errors*
> *with grace, for this is one way*
> *that our souls grow."*

In my book *Guideposts to Happiness*,* I talked about ways we can live with lightheartedness and selflessness, and one of the ways was taking things with grace. Nowadays, it's become rare to find people who can take things with grace. I've found that modern people often tend to find excuses and reasons to justify themselves; they find self-reflection difficult to practice and are given to explaining themselves rather than changing themselves. It may be the product of modern schooling and later experiences in the world, but whatever the cause may be, many people today share this tendency to find excuses. We've become smarter, and that has led us to habitually attach reasons to things and lose sight of our humility.

If you have noticed a growing habit of finding excuses and justifying yourself, please remember to take things with grace as

---

* Ryuho Okawa, *Guideposts to Happiness* (New York: IRH Press, 2015).

the first way of living lightheartedly and selflessly. As human be-ings, we cannot help but make mistakes in life, so when we do, we should strive to accept our errors with grace, for this is one way that our souls grow. When we fail to accept our wrongs with grace, we won't be able to take a step forward on our journey of life.

There used to be a time when the ability to accept things with grace was valued and talked about by everyone, but in these recent times, people no longer think deeply about this quality. It seems to have become the stuff of olden ideals. But I believe that it's important for all of us to engrave into our hearts even just the idea of taking things with grace.

*"Through diligence, you will nurture a personality as natural as a passing breeze."*

The second way of living lightheartedly and selflessly is to prac-tice giving love to many people without any expectation of return. The number of people who practice this attitude is so small—less than one in a hundred—but you're certain to find these people around you if you look very closely.

The starting point, then, is to decide to follow their example and aim to become one of them. When you see people in the morning, wish them a good morning, but vanish as lightly as a breeze, as if you were laying a flower blossom on their lapel and then vanishing instantly. Through diligence, you will nurture a personality as natural as a passing breeze. I hope that you will strive to cultivate this personality.

> *"Human life is finite in one sense but eternal in another sense."*

The third way of living with lightheartedness is to know that human life is finite in one sense but eternal in another sense. This may sound a lot like a Zen koan, so I will explain what it means. Human life is indeed finite, because our days are always numbered: at the shortest, we have several years of life in this world remaining, and at the longest, several decades. We may find some rare exceptions, but anyone who is alive at this moment will most likely be gone a hundred years later. Not a single one of your family members, friends, or neighbors will be around that far into the future.

Looking at human life in this way inspires us to feel sympathy toward the people around us and to realize that we share the same fate. Several decades from now, we will no longer be in this world and will have moved on to the afterlife. My teachings promise you that life after death exists. And if we're all destined to be gone from this world eventually, it's only natural to wish to leave behind something precious in the hearts of as many people as possible.

Just as every person's face is unique, we each have a unique heart leading to a different realm of the other world. There are very few people who return to the exact same world as those around them. Out of a thousand people, a handful may be returning to similar neighborhoods of the other world, while the rest are bound for other places, meaning they will seldom see one another. When we think about this, it's only natural to want to treasure every encounter we have while we're in this world and to wish to leave each person with the impression of us as a fresh breeze in May.

> *"Knowing we're given infinite opportunities for another chance allows us to live lightheartedly and selflessly, as well as with grace."*

Life is also infinite. Having infinite life means having an unending number of second chances in life. This is indeed a great expression of God's love.

When we think about life after death, the possibility of falling to hell in the afterlife is a frightening and devastating thought. But even if you end up in the world of hell, your soul will never be destroyed, and this is a truth we feel thankful for. This means that even if we fail the test that is our earthly life, we can still strive to improve our grades, and we'll be given a chance to eventually score a passing grade.

If human souls that fell to hell were truly destined to perish, most human souls would cease to exist at some point in the cycle of their reincarnations.

Finding yourself in hell is a truly terrible thing to happen. But seen from another standpoint, it means that you're allowed to continue to exist even though you didn't earn a passing grade. And what's more, you're always given the chance to rise to heaven by undergoing several hundred years or so of spiritual training in hell. And then, after your time in heaven, you're given another chance to be reborn into this world on Earth. There is little that could deserve more gratitude.

In fact, it's very difficult to fail every single incarnation. If you were able to do this, it would be a sign of great determination! But even then, you would always have another chance.

If your actions toward someone sowed bad karma in a past life, you may decide to be born again, among the same people and in the same time and place on Earth, for a chance to redeem the wrongs you committed. The person you hurt may choose to be born as a member of your family, a friend, or someone else in your life, and former enemies also meet each other on Earth very frequently.

In this way, we're given many chances to try again. Knowing we're given infinite opportunities for another chance allows us to live lightheartedly and selflessly, as well as with grace. When we don't know that we have more than one life to live, we might feel that we're in constant danger of committing wrongs that we'll regret for eternity, and that might lead us to live in unsightly ways. But the truth is that we don't just have second chances; we're given third chances, fourth chances, and further chances continuing on into eternity.

Some people's impression of reincarnation is eternal misery. But the truth is that it's a form of mercy that gives our souls a chance to keep living, even though we continue to make mistakes. It's important to take this broad perspective on life and be thankful. With this view of our lives in our hearts, we'll see that there is no better way to live life than to live with lightheartedness and selflessness.

# AFTERWORD

This book is sprinkled with a plethora of keys to success in life. As you pore over these pages every now and then, you'll receive the inspirations that you'll need at that time.

I hope that you will keep this book by your side throughout your life and use it as a source of power to transform yourself and contribute to the creation of Utopia in this world.

Ryuho Okawa
Founder and CEO
Happy Science

The contents of this book were compiled based on translations of Ryuho Okawa's Q&A sessions featured in *The Liberty*, a Japanese monthly magazine published by IRH Press (http://eng.the-liberty.com). Following is a list of the dates of publication of the original articles each of the book's chapters is based on.

## Chapter 1   How to Build Mental Toughness

I.  The Art of Mastering Relationships
   1  Learning from Other People's Advice and
      Opinions: November 1999
   2  Respecting Boundaries: October 1999
   3  Developing the Power of Persuasion: July 2000

II.  The Art of Actualizing Your Dreams and Ideals
   4  Developing Your Capabilities: September 2006
   5  Shifting the Course of Your Destiny: April 2000
   6  Persevering through Hardship: June 2002

III.  The Art of Building Mental Strength
   7  Deepening Your Understanding of Difficult Subjects: June 1999
   8  Examining Our Inner Selves Spiritually: March 2000
   9  Dealing with Jealousy and Criticism: February 1998

## Chapter 2   How to Become an Influential Leader

I. The Art of Surviving in a Tough World
   10  The Source of Leadership: February–March 2001
   11  The Principle of Market Survival: October–November 2002
   12  The Makings of Legendary Figures: March 1999

## Chapter 3  How to Overcome Stress

# ABOUT THE AUTHOR

**Ryuho Okawa** is the founder and CEO of a global movement, Happy Science, and international best-selling author with a simple goal: to help people find true happiness and create a better world.

His deep compassion and sense of responsibility for the happiness of each individual has prompted him to deliver more than 2,800 lectures (over 120 in English) and publish over 2,400 titles of religious, spiritual, and self-development teachings, covering a broad range of topics including how our thoughts influence reality, the nature of love, and the path to enlightenment. Eastern wisdom that Okawa offers helps us find a new avenue for solutions to the issues we are facing personally and globally now. He also writes on the topics of management and economy, as well as the relationship between religion and politics in the global context. To date, Okawa's books have sold over 100 million copies worldwide and been translated into 30 languages.

Okawa has dedicated himself to improving society and creating a better world. In 1986, Okawa founded Happy Science as a spiritual movement dedicated to bringing greater happiness to humankind by uniting religions and cultures to live in harmony. Happy Science has grown rapidly from its beginnings in Japan to a worldwide organization with over 12 million members in more than 100 countries. Okawa is compassionately committed to the spiritual growth of others. In addition to writing and publishing books, he continues to give lectures around the world.

# ABOUT HAPPY SCIENCE

Happy Science is a global movement that empowers individuals to find purpose and spiritual happiness and to share that happiness with their families, societies, and the world. With more than twelve million members around the world, Happy Science aims to increase awareness of spiritual truths and expand our capacity for love, compassion, and joy so that together we can create the kind of world we all wish to live in.

Activities at Happy Science are based on the Principles of Happiness (Love, Wisdom, Self-Reflection, and Progress). These principles embrace worldwide philosophies and beliefs, transcending boundaries of culture and religions.

LOVE teaches us to give ourselves freely without expecting anything in return; it encompasses giving, nurturing, and forgiving.

WISDOM leads us to the insights of spiritual truths, and opens us to the true meaning of life and the will of God (the universe, the highest power, Buddha).

SELF-REFLECTION brings a mindful, nonjudgmental lens to our thoughts and actions to help us find our truest selves—the essence of our souls—and deepen our connection to the highest power. It helps us attain a clean and peaceful mind and leads us to the right life path.

PROGRESS emphasizes the positive, dynamic aspects of our spiritual growth—actions we can take to manifest and spread happiness around the world. It's a path that not only expands our soul growth, but also furthers the collective potential of the world we live in.

# PROGRAMS AND EVENTS

The doors of Happy Science are open to all. We offer a variety of programs and events, including self-exploration and self-growth programs, spiritual seminars, meditation and contemplation sessions, study groups, and book events. Our programs are designed to:

- Deepen your understanding of your purpose and meaning in life
- Improve your relationships and increase your capacity to love unconditionally
- Attain peace of mind, decrease anxiety and stress, and feel positive
- Gain deeper insights and a broader perspective on the world
- Learn how to overcome life's challenges

… and much more.

# INTERNATIONAL SEMINARS

Each year, friends from all over the world join our international seminars, held at our faith centers in Japan. Different programs are offered each year and cover a wide variety of topics, including improving relationships, practicing the Eightfold Path to enlightenment, and loving yourself, to name just a few.

# HAPPY SCIENCE MONTHLY

Our monthly publication covers the latest featured lectures, members' life-changing experiences and other news from members around the world, book reviews, and many other topics. Downloadable PDF files are available at **happyscience-na.org**. Copies and back issues in Portuguese, Chinese, and other languages are available upon request. For more information, contact us via e-mail at **tokyo@happy-science.org**. For more information, visit **happyscience-na.org** or **happyscience.org**.

# CONTACT INFORMATION

Happy Science is a worldwide organization with faith centers around the globe. For a comprehensive list of centers, visit the worldwide directory at happy-science.org. The following are some of the many Happy Science locations:

## UNITED STATES AND CANADA

**New York**
79 Franklin St.,
New York, NY 10013
Phone: 212-343-7972
Fax: 212-343-7973
Email: ny@happy-science.org
Website: happyscience-na.org

**New Jersey**
725 River Rd, #102B,
Edgewater, NJ 07020
Phone: 201-313-0127
Fax: 201-313-0120
Email: nj@happy-science.org
Website: happyscience-na.org

**Florida**
5208 8thSt.
Zephyrhills,
FL 33542
Phone: 813-715-0000
Fax: 813-715-0010
Email: florida@happy-science.org
Website: happyscience-na.org

**Atlanta**
1874 Piedmont Ave., NE
Suite 360-C
Atlanta, GA 30324
Phone: 404-892-7770
Email: atlanta@happy-science.org
Website: happyscience-na.org

**San Francisco**
525 Clinton St.
Redwood City, CA 94062
Phone & Fax: 650-363-2777
Email: sf@happy-science.org
Website: happyscience-na.org

**Los Angeles**
1590 E. Del Mar Blvd.,
Pasadena, CA 91106
Phone: 626-395-7775
Fax: 626-395-7776
Email: la@happy-science.org
Website: happyscience-na.org

**Orange County**
10231 Slater Ave., #204
Fountain Valley, CA 92708
Phone: 714-745-1140
Email: oc@happy-science.org
Website: happyscience-na.org

## San Diego

7841 Balboa Ave., Suite #202
San Diego, CA 92111
Phone: 619-381-7615
Fax: 626-395-7776
E-mail: sandiego@happy-science.org
Website: happyscience-na.org

## Hawaii

Phone: 808-591-9772
Fax: 808-591-9776
Email: hi@happy-science.org
Website: happyscience-na.org

## Kauai

4504 Kukui Street,
Dragon Building 21, Kapaa, HI 96746
Phone: 808-822-7007
Fax: 808-822-6007
Email: kauai-hi@happy-science.org
Website: happyscience-na.org

## Toronto

845 The Queensway
Etobicoke ON M8Z 1N6 Canada
Phone: 1-416-901-3747
Email: toronto@happy-science.org
Website: happy-science.ca

## Vancouver

#212-2609 East 49th Avenue
Vancouver, BC, V5S 1J9, Canada
Phone: 1-604-437-7735
Fax: 1-604-437-7764
Email: vancouver@happy-science.org
Website: happy-science.ca

# INTERNATIONAL

## Tokyo

1-6-7 Togoshi, Shinagawa
Tokyo, 142-0041 Japan
Phone: 81-3-6384-5770
Fax: 81-3-6384-5776
Email: tokyo@happy-science.org
Website: happy-science.org

## London

3 Margaret St.
London, W1W 8RE
United Kingdom
Phone: 44-20-7323-9255
Fax: 44-20-7323-9344
Email: eu@happy-science.org
Website: happyscience-uk.org

## Sydney

516 Pacific Hwy, Lane Cove North,
NSW 2066, Australia
Phone: 61-2-9411-2877
Fax: 61-2-9411-2822
Email: sydney@happy-science.org
Website: happy-science.org.au

## South Sao Paulo

Rua. Domingos de Morais 1154,
Vila Mariana, Sao Paulo-SP
CEP 04009-002, Brazil
Phone: 55-11-5088-3800
Fax: 55-11-5088-3806
Email: sp@happy-science.org
Website: happy-science.com.br

## Jundiai

Rua Congo, 447, Jd. Bonfiglioli
Jundiai-CEP, 13207-340, Brazil
Phone: 55-11-4587-5952
Email: jundiai@happy-science.org

## Seoul

74, Sadang-ro 27-gil,
Dongjak-gu, Seoul, Korea
Phone: 82-2-3478-8777
Fax: 82-2- 3478-9777
Email: korea@happy-science.org
Website: happyscience-korea.org

## Taipei

No. 89, Lane 155, Dunhua N. Road
Songshan District,
Taipei City 105, Taiwan
Phone: 886-2-2719-9377
Fax: 886-2-2719-5570
Email: taiwan@happy-science.org
Website: happyscience-tw.org

## Malaysia

No 22A, Block 2, Jalil Link Jalan Jalil
Jaya 2, Bukit Jalil 57000, Kuala Lumpur,
Malaysia
Phone: 60-3-8998-7877
Fax: 60-3-8998-7977
Email: malaysia@happy-science.org
Website: happyscience.org.my

## Nepal

Kathmandu Metropolitan City
Ward No. 15, Ring Road, Kimdol,
Sitapaila
Kathmandu, Nepal
Phone: 977-1-427-2931
Email: nepal@happy-science.org

## Uganda

Plot 877 Rubaga Road,
Kampala
P.O. Box 34130,
Kampala, Uganda
Phone: 256-79-3238-002
Email: uganda@happy-science.org
Website: happyscience-uganda.org

# ABOUT IRH PRESS USA

IRH Press USA Inc. was founded in 2013 as an affiliated firm of IRH Press Co., Ltd. Based in New York, the press publishes books in various categories including spirituality, religion, and self-improvement and publishes books by Ryuho Okawa, the author of 100 million books sold worldwide. For more information, visit OkawaBooks.com.

Follow us on:
Facebook: OkawaBooks
Twitter: OkawaBooks
Goodreads: RyuhoOkawa
Instagram: OkawaBooks
Pinterest: OkawaBooks

# BOOKS BY RYUHO OKAWA

## THE STRONG MIND

The Art of Building the Inner Strength
to Overcome Life's Difficulties

Softcover | 192 pages | $15.95 |
ISBN-10: 1942125364
ISBN-13: 978-1942125365

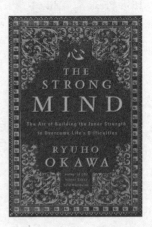

In *The Strong Mind*, author Ryuho Okawa presents a self-transformative perspective on life's hardships and challenges as precious opportunities for our inner growth. No matter what your circumstances or how slow your progress may seem, you will develop the strength of character to rise above the limitations that each stage of life can bring. With this book as your guide, life's challenges will become treasures that bring lasting and continuous enrichment for your soul.

## THE LAWS OF INVINCIBLE LEADERSHIP

An Empowering Guide for Continuous and
Lasting Success in Business and in Life

Hardcover | 224 pages | $19.95 |
ISBN-10: 1942125305
ISBN-13: 978-1942125303

Ryuho Okawa shares essential principles for all who wish to become invincible managers and leaders in their fields of work, organizations, societies, and nations. Let Okawa's breakthrough management philosophy in this empowering guide help you find the seeds of your future success. Your keys to becoming an invincible overall winner in life and in business are just pages away.

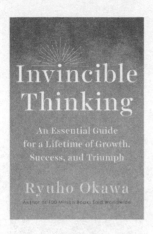

## INVINCIBLE THINKING

An Essential Guide for a Lifetime of
Growth, Success, and Triumph

Hardcover | 208 pages | $16.95 |
ISBN-10: 1942125259
ISBN-13: 978-1942125259

*Invincible Thinking* is the dynamite that lets us open a crack of possibility in a mountain of difficulties, the powerful drill that lets us tunnel through the solid rock of complacency and defeatism and move steadily ahead toward triumph. A mindset of invincibility is your most powerful inner tool for transforming any event or circumstance into inner wisdom and soul growth. Invincible thinking will give you all the nourishment you'll ever need to fulfill your purpose in life and become a guiding light for others.

## THE LAWS OF SUCCESS

A Spiritual Guide to Turning Your Hopes
into Reality

Softcover | 208 pages | $15.95 |
ISBN-10: 1942125151
ISBN-13: 978-1942125150

*The Laws of Success* offers 8 spiritual principles that, when put to practice in our day-to-day life, will help us attain lasting success and let us experience the fulfillment of living our purpose and the joy of sharing our happiness with many others. The timeless wisdom and practical steps that Okawa offers will guide us through any difficulties and problems we may face in life, and serve as guiding principles for living a positive, constructive, and meaningful life.

# THINK BIG!

## Be Positive and Be Brave to Achieve Your Dreams

Softcover | 160 pages | $12.95 |
ISBN-10: 1942125046
ISBN-13: 978-1942125044

This self-development book offers practical steps to consciously create a life of rewarding challenge, fulfillment, and achievement. Using his own life experiences and wisdom as the roadmap, Ryuho Okawa inspires us with practical steps for building courage, choosing a constructive perspective, finding a true calling, cultivating awareness, and harnessing our personal power to realize our dreams.

# THE HEART OF WORK

## 10 Keys to Living Your Calling

Softcover | 224 pages | $12.95 |
ISBN-10: 1942125038
ISBN-13: 978-1942125037

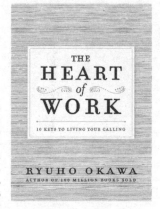

Ryuho Okawa shares 10 key philosophies and goals to live by to guide us through our work lives and triumphantly live our calling. There are key principles that will help you get to the heart of work, manage your time well, prioritize your work, live with long health and vitality, achieve growth, and more. People of all walks of life from the businessperson, executive, artist, teacher, mother, to even students, and more will find the keys to achieving happiness and success in their special calling.

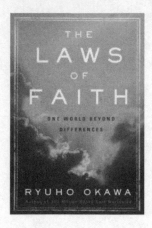

## THE LAWS OF FAITH

### One World Beyond Differences

Softcover | 208 pages | $15.95 |
ISBN-10: 1942125348
ISBN-13: 978-1942125341

Ryuho Okawa preaches at the core of a new universal religion from various angles while integrating logical and spiritual viewpoints in mind with current world situations. This book offers us the key to accept diversities beyond differences in ethnicity, religion, race, gender, descent, and so on, harmonize the individuals and nations and create a world filled with peace and prosperity.

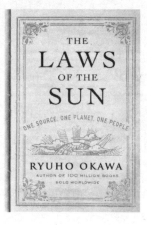

## THE LAWS OF THE SUN

### One Source, One Planet, One People

Softcover | 288 pages | $15.95 |
ISBN-10: 1942125437
ISBN-13: 978-1942125433

Imagine if you could ask God why he created this world and what spiritual laws he used to shape us—and everything around us. In *The Laws of the Sun*, Okawa outlines these laws of the universe and provides a road map for living one's life with greater purpose and meaning. This powerful book shows the way to realize true happiness—a happiness that continues from this world through the other.

# BOOKS BY RYUHO OKAWA

## THE CHALLENGE OF THE MIND
An Essential Guide to Buddha's Teachings:
Zen, Karma, and Enlightenment

## MY JOURNEY THROUGH THE SPIRIT WORLD
A True Account of My Experiences of the Hereafter

## THE STARTING POINT OF HAPPINESS
An Inspiring Guide to Positive Living with
Faith, Love, and Courage

## A LIFE OF TRIUMPH
Unleashing Your Light Upon the World

## THE MIRACLE OF MEDITATION
Opening Your Life to Peace, Joy, and the Power Within

## HEALING FROM WITHIN
Life-Changing Keys to Calm, Spiritual, and Healthy Living

## THE UNHAPPINESS SYNDROME
28 Habits of Unhappy People (and How to Change Them)

## INVITATION TO HAPPINESS
7 Inspirations from Your Inner Angel

## MESSAGES FROM HEAVEN
What Jesus, Buddha, Muhammad, and Moses Would Say Today

## THE LAWS OF MISSION
Essential Truths for Spiritual Awakening in a Secular Age

## THE LAWS OF JUSTICE
How We Can Solve World Conflicts and Bring Peace

## SECRETS OF THE EVERLASTING TRUTHS
A New Paradigm for Living on Earth

## THE MOMENT OF TRUTH
Become a Living Angel Today

## THE NINE DIMENSIONS
Unveiling the Laws of Eternity

## THE MYSTICAL LAWS
Going Beyond the Dimensional Boundaries

## CHANGE YOUR LIFE, CHANGE THE WORLD
A Spiritual Guide to Living Now

---

For a complete list of books, visit OkawaBooks.com

---